Changing Planes

By

Kathy Scott

Illustrations by Kim Mellema

Alder Creek Publishing

Copyright 2008 by Kathy Scott
First Edition/First Printing

ALL RIGHTS RESERVED. No part of this book may be reproduced in any manner without the express written consent of the publisher, except in the case of brief excerpts in reviews and articles. All inquiries should be addressed to Alder Creek Publishing, 1178 Valleyview Drive, Hastings, MI 49058 –

Printed in The United States of America

Illustrations by Kim Mellema
Typesetting and technical design by Daniel Terpstra & John Crowley
Editing advisor, Johannah Oster

10 9 8 7 6 5 4 3 2 1

Scott, Kathy J., 1954-
    Changing Planes / Kathy Scott

    ISBN (Hardcover) 978-0-9657663-4-0

    Copyright 2008
    1. Outdoor Life   2. Natural History   3. Nature Writing
    4. Fly Fishing   5. Journals, diaries, and memoirs

I. Title
799.124

Also by Kathy Scott,
    Moose in the Water / Bamboo on the Bench
    Headwaters Fall as Snow

Introduction

Life is filled with choices. We can live out our lives in quiet desperation or embrace life searching for and discovering new paths, paths which lead to new experiences. In the following pages the reader will discover that Kathy Scott is one of those memorable individuals who cautiously but steadfastly moves through life knowing full well that things do not stay the same. As a graduate student in the 70s I studied futurism, read Toffler, a predictor of the woes of too much change too soon. Kathy Scott, in *Changing Planes*, provides a more benign yet equally challenging view of change. Kathy's view is one of choice rather than happenstance. Change not for the worse but refreshingly for the better.

Changing Planes is Kathy Scott's latest work, preceded by *Headwaters Fall as Snow* and *Moose in the Water, Bamboo on the Bench*. In this, the third of her trilogy, she shares how her life has been altered by involvement in the split cane community and environmental issues. Anglers and advocates brought together by a timeless appreciation for craftsmanship is Kathy's theme. In *Changing Planes* she weaves her theme as deftly as she furls a silk leader.

So much of what we read today concerning the out-of-doors is written in terms of the "Hook and Bullet" essayist or the purveyors of competitive angling. Kathy Scott, like a 21st century "Lady Leopold" walks a different trail, blending nature with science, craftsmanship with caring and she does it quite well. I wish there were more writers like Kathy and I wish the world would take her message to heart.

~ Ron Barch

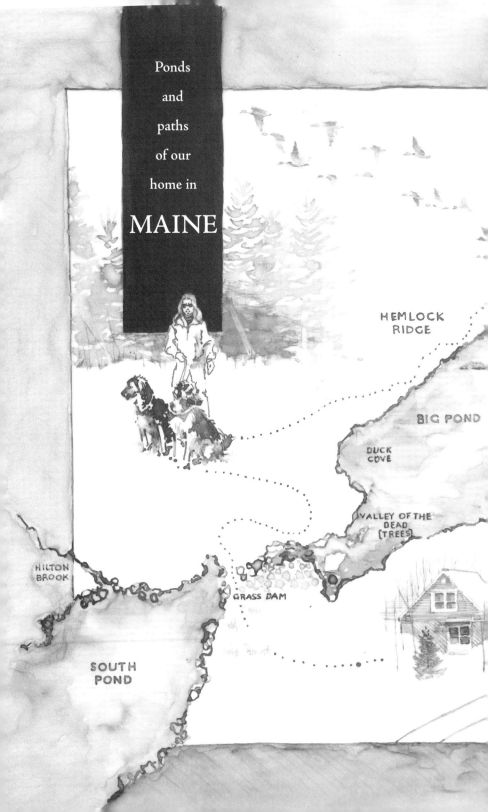

"The future is not some place we are going to,
but one we are creating. The paths are not to be found,
but made, and the activity of making them,
changes both the maker and the destination"

~ John Schaar

Changing Planes

Sunday, November 16

*M*oose tracks. An early dusting of snow made them visible, even by moonlight, even before they passed through the light coming from the shop window. I paused there in the chill night, content that all was well with my outside world, and watched David work at his bench just inside. Clarity comes with November, a month at the edge of change, when all of life is so simple. For the moose, stay sheltered from the cold and find food for the winter. For David, glide the hand plane along a tapered strip of bamboo held securely on his workbench. He needed only to shave the cane, measure, and pass the plane again. Nothing else tonight -maybe scratch Kodiak behind the ears if he stirred away from his dog bed near the woodstove. That did not look likely at the moment. Sheltered here under the silhouettes of white pine, life becomes very safe and very clear. I tapped on the window and waved to his smile, then joined him inside.

After several years of living in a rodmaker's shop, almost literally, cane shavings become a welcome part of life, beautiful golden curls, nesting material. The aroma of bamboo flamed along the length of the culm becomes the fragrance of sweet grass, cleansing to the soul. Any day out in the world, however hectic and frustrating, can be snuffed into insignificance by an evening immersed in the gentle craft of shaping the lovely reed. All is again right with the world.

Kathy Scott

The leftover splits David set aside from past rods caught my eye, and I found myself looking them over, admiring their straightness, counting them. Six in one bundle, eight in the other. Such a shame to let them stand there, wonderful raw strips. Enough for a single tip two-piece rod, maybe a little rod, a beautiful tortoise flamed fly rod for a beautiful brook trout stream. Little Labrador, or the South Branch of the Au Sable, maybe.

The feeling was suddenly clear. I should take the next step. After years of a partnership and, in effect, apprenticeship, wonderful hours as a shop elf and assistant in rodmaking and rodmaking classes, after working with strips of cane, getting to know them, strengthening a vision for their evolving future, finally my own vision had evolved.

I asked David, "Do you have any plans for these strips?" I couldn't look away from them, I wanted them so much. But they were his, and I didn't want to influence his answer. Maybe he needed them. He is a friend too dear to deny me; I'm too good a friend to insist.

"Not really. They're just the extras I didn't need. Why?" He paused in his planing to walk to the corner where I stood admiring the splits.

"I was thinking about making them into a little rod," I said. "Just a single tip, small stream rod. Think they'd be okay for that?"

David would never doubt for a moment that I could do it, although maybe he should. I knew exactly what I was proposing: sixty hours of work for myself, a like amount of guidance, sharing equipment, and patience from him. Chances were good that

Changing Planes

neither one of us would make any progress on the long list of repairs necessary to convert this, the second, older house turned rod shop back into a finished home. We had borrowed the money to annex more of our watershed, but this house came with it, a string attached. There would also be less of an immediate chance that we'd transform the little house we built originally, just south through the pines, into a homey and efficient rod shop. Two dreams on delay, not that waiting for things of importance bothers either one of us. Still, it wasn't a light proposition.

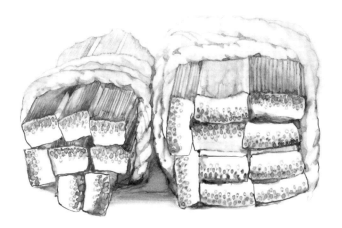

David picked up one bundle of splits, looked them over, refreshed his memory, and then picked up the other. "They're all butt strips, but that doesn't matter. It just has to do with node spacing closer together on the butt of the culm. On a small rod, say, a Garrison 193 like the one of Al's; you'd be likely to have a couple of nodes, anyway. These would be fine."

Kathy Scott

Garrison 193, I thought. I loved Al Medved's rod. The people of my cane world, the rodmakers, are as special to me as the rods they make. It is our honor to possess a rod from a friend who not only is one of the very best makers, but who also rarely, if ever, sells a rod. I sometimes think of Al Medved as a living metaphor for this generation of rodmakers, a generous, caring community. His modest good nature shines through the praise and insights he shares freely whenever cane people gather. Years ago, he was the first to compliment David on his first rod; a beginning maker cherishes honest support. We'd all been together at a rodmakers' gathering on Michigan's Au Sable when he'd offered us the 193. I fished it on the South Branch just last July. So sweet, so perfect.

I grinned. "Garrison didn't flame his rods, though." These leftover strips had been flamed a dark brown in the culm before the rough splitting.

David smiled back. "He wouldn't hold it against you."

David always seems to be a little amazed at the trivia I've picked up these years. A Garrison 193 indicates the maker who originated the taper of that fly rod, Everett Garrison, and his designated model number. 193 refers to .193 of an inch, the measurement of the rod fifty inches from the tip; not all rod models are so easily deciphered. There's a system for plotting and understanding the stress curves of all the tapers, but I'm just glad to have handled so many that I've memorized their actions. For me, it's more of an intuitive thing. Rodmaking - some say closer to religion, certainly spiritual, a fine line.

Changing Planes

It was late, though. There was little time left to do more than walk home through the pines and the sounds of a November night. We stopped in the moonlight, David, Kodiak, and I, listening for geese coming in from the north. Some kinds of deep happiness make moments into song.

Kathy Scott

Saturday, November 22

Right from the start it was clear: rodmaking is a process, not an event. Over the week, David printed the taper for me, graphed to show a visual representation of the action, and we planned for the beginning. I decided that I wanted to soak the scavenged strips before heating and straightening them, before displacing the remnants of the nodes. We would need a piece of PVC pipe, capped at one end. The strips would be lightly bound and immersed in water for a few days, easier, then, to work, softer. Flooring is made from bamboo - it's very hard.

That was tonight's project, making the tank for immersing the strips, after we finished stacking the wood in the winter woodpile, after walking Kodiak around the ponds, after running a week's worth of errands in one Saturday. The strips were five and one half feet long; a tank would need to be six feet in length. We examined them again.

Look how straight these are already." David demonstrated sighting down the strip. "This bend here appears at first to be at the node, but it's just before it. There's another bend just after the node."

Tonkin cane grows quickly with nodes, dams, for support as it reaches skyward, forty feet in a season. He passed the strip to me, and I sighted along it. Hmm. Not so obvious. I redirected the strip, aiming for the bright window, and David touched the bends to help me see them.

"If you bend a strip right at the node, you'll have a better chance of breaking it," he cautioned. "I take the major sweeping bends out first, and then inspect the strip again to see what's left."

I put the strip down on the cold flat surface of the kitchen's wood-burning cook stove, cast iron and largely unused but handy at the moment. I spread out its five mates and the eight from the other bundle. David handed me a tape measure, and we looked at the node spacing. I hoped the eight could be tip strips, giving me two extra strips to guard against disaster when working with the fine tip dimensions. Only six would need to survive my attempts to plane them fine enough.

David had originally marked a red diagonal line across the strips of one bundle, a blue diagonal across the other, but he couldn't remember if the line was toward the top, tip, or bottom, butt, of the culm of bamboo. Since the nodes are closer together nearer the ground, I laid the extended tape measure along the strips and locked it in place. The red set of strips had node spacings of thirteen inches, then fourteen, then fifteen. The red line marked the end with the thirteen-inch spacing, the butt, the end closest to the ground. The blue line was also nearest the butt end of the other set of strips. David considered the spacing while I waited.

"Looks like the nodes of the red strips would fall right to make a Garrison 193 tapered rod." I waited for him to continue. "The blue strips would be fine for the tip. The nodes would fall four inches from both the top and the ferrule."

Perfect. No potential trouble spots at either the rod's tip or where the two sections of the rod would join together. Using the blue strips for the tip meant I'd have two extra as safeguards for the section with the most exacting work during the long process ahead. The tips would be so tiny, so thin. It was hard to imagine that I could find enough skill to prevent ruining at least one.

David was measuring the total length, and then judging the diameter we'd need for the soak tube by bunching all of the strips together. Soaking is probably more common with blond strips since the water protects against discoloration from the direct heat applied to the strip during straightening. For me, it was more important that soaking would make straightening easier, like an internal steam treatment. These strips were already a rich mottled brown from the original flaming.

"Why can't we just cut them to length now?" I asked. It seemed logical: shorter soaking tube needed, fewer nodes overall to pinch and straighten. Each strip had four nodes; I'd only need the length containing two.

"We could cut them, but we'd have no insurance. What if a strip breaks or splits? You could just stagger that part if you keep the entire strip at this point. What if you break a butt strip? You only have six."

I could see his points.

We drove to town after dark and picked up six feet of three-inch diameter PVC plus end caps and a couple other pieces. By the time we drove home, every star I'd ever seen was out. While we roused Kodiak from the south house, Orion the Winter Hunter chased the Pleiades, the ever-elusive flock of geese, into the sky. Kodes sampled the night air, his home as our constant companion since the day he captured our hearts at the animal shelter and moved in to chase ever elusive geese of his own. Winter, his favorite. What few husky genes he had were well beyond diluting. We worked at the north house just long enough to glue on the bottom end cap for waterproofing the soak tube, then walked Kodiak back home to the south house following the broad path of the Milky Way.

Sunday, November 23

This morning was bathed in low-angle sunlight under a seamless blue November sky. The frost disappeared quickly. Unusual warming had melted the early ice off the ponds, and the hundred Canada geese which had come in just at dusk became restless with the morning. We heard the honking start and ran outside as it grew more urgent, more agitated. Then we watched a hundred pairs of wings lift the V into formation, bank hard, and continue south in their excitement.

I was excited, too.

We ate a quick breakfast, then Kodiak led us through the towering white pines to the north house. David aroused a fire from the coals, and I arranged my strips again to look them over.

"These nodes are pretty flat already," I observed. David agreed. His early work had saved me a little time on these leftover strips. He always rough files the nodes on the entire culm before flaming it. If the nodes were filed after flaming, the torch's effects would be filed right back off to a blond spot. Forethought. Handy for me now, too.

He held the tube while I bit my lip and poured in three large glasses of water. Then I bundled the butt strips with a red rubber band and fed them into the tube. I bundled the tip strips with a blue rubber band and worked them in beside the red. They were almost all the way in when the water splashed out and on to my feet. We both jumped and laughed at how serious I'd been.

Forethought. Less water. Water after strips.

David poured some of the water out while I sopped the excess off the floor; then we slipped the tip strips the rest of the way in. The tube was heavy; its open top taller than my head, but David could look inside.

"They're all submerged," he said. "Where should we lean this tube?"

We discussed it quickly and decided on the bathtub. With the shower door's railing running across the top, the tube couldn't fall over.

We passed the early afternoon walking with Kodiak around the ponds, almost deserted now, just a single great blue heron. We wished it a timely and safe departure for the south. The black surface of the ponds was as smooth as glass, a mirror reflecting the beaver lodge, the black spruce and balsam fir along the shore.

Changing Planes

As the afternoon waned, David planed strips for Hutch and Sean. Our habit is to refer to rods in progress by the names of those waiting, a useful reference and a reminder of the close relationship with the people involved. Hutch, Chris Hutchins; we coach the high school fly fishing club together. Sean is the president of our Trout Unlimited chapter. While David planed, I slipped though the pines with Kodiak to take clothes off the line, maybe the last outdoor drying of the season. We had had two weeks of snow by this time last year.

Kodiak made a fuss as we crossed back though the pines toward the clearing at the north house. I struggled to interpret until I heard water splashing down below, in the direction of the ponds. We crept to the water's edge and scanned the far shore until we saw the moose. We froze as it lifted its head above the water, then, when its head submerged to resume eating, I risked a radio alert to David.

"Moose," I whispered into the handset. "Moose just across the point from the deck."

There was a pause. I pictured David moving from his bench to the deck.

"It's a bull," David's voice came back.

He'd seen it, so Kodiak and I risked retreating and the dash through the woods to join him on the deck. The moose had a small but significant rack. He continued inspecting the shallows for edibles before wandering to the shore, then back into the water again. We stood in silence, listening to the small splashes he made, watching the setting November sun dance red highlights through his coat. When he nuzzled the water, the second moose, his perfect reflection, came up to nuzzle the air.

Finally, it was too dark to see anything but the silver flashes of disturbed water he made as he shuffled.

"I'll go look in on your cane," David whispered, and I followed him indoors. The strips were floating up a little, so we drilled holes in a smaller PVC cap which could be inserted into the tube above the strips to hold them under the water. David held the doctored end cap so we could see the holes. "Going with a theme," he said. Six holes, a hexagon, like the shape of a cane rod.

I stood on a stool and placed the holey cap in the tube and then put an appropriately sized cap over the end to hold the spacer and the strips in place. A teaspoon of bleach might be a good thought, too. The water would smell better later. We'd see.

David stoked the woodstove, and Kodiak curled up on his bed in front of it. David started planing again on one side of him. On the other, I switched on my little bench light and started to make some fishing leaders, furled fly fishing leaders. It's a useful craft worth saving, simple, time-tested, but at risk of being lost like too many good things. Cane rods, for instance. Just infinitely easier to make. By the time Kodiak was snoring, I'd finished two, and they were hanging from the beam above me. David had one more tip strip to plane before he'd stop to sharpen his blade. I put some music on; David stopped to add a log to the fire.

"Want to check your strips?" he asked.

Changing Planes

We both laughed. I did, but I wouldn't admit it.

Tomorrow, we'll order my plane.

THURSDAY NOVEMBER 27TH
Thanksgiving Morning

I tried every trick I could for two hours, but I couldn't get back to sleep. At 4:45, I thought of slipping out unnoticed - impossible- but something to think about while the clock ticked toward dawn. Impossible, I reasoned, because David always knows what I'm up to. It's one of those things in life I can count on. Tuesday, for instance, should have been a work day like every other work day, David leaving his desk and e-mail from 11 until noon. I had watched the clock during my lunch a few miles away. At 11:05, I'd quickly e-mailed J. D. Wagner, Rodmakers, really Jeff Wagner and Casimira Orlowski, to request a surprise planing form for David for Christmas. My strategic timing should have allowed time for a response and deletion of the entire transaction before David would return, but when I had checked for Jeff or Casimira's response at 11:30, the "read" box on our e-mail had been activated. David, who never swaps his lunch time, had.

Chances were good that I'd disturb him if I moved. If there was any question, Kodiak would tip him off anyway. So I tried to think of something boring; nothing came to mind. By 5:15, when the alarm clocks normally start their cascade from the first clock's "it's getting toward morning" to the last's "better get up now," I got up, Thanksgiving or not. I checked the e-mail while munching breakfast. Kodiak had snuggled in next to David, taking more than half the room. Rare that I'd be up before David, much more rare that I'd be active before Kodiak. I left a two-way radio near them, switched mine on, and followed the beam of my headlamp through the frosty air to the north house.

David, Kodiak, the frosty air, these woods.

I have a lot to be thankful for.

I have a best friend in the truest sense of the word and have shared lives with him for a very long time. We are graced with an animal friend who trades unconditional devotion for romps outdoors and a modicum of patience. We have extended, supportive families that we love. David has a friend he can call from anywhere at any time and talk for hours; I have a friend who sends me poetry and inspires me to do my best. We are fortunate to live at the edge of Maine's Great North Woods and pass our mornings watching geese excite themselves into flight again, our evenings watching beavers swim close to investigate us, our nights under a full moon, or brilliant stars, or waving green and red northern lights, or rare and precious comets, or...

We have a lot to be thankful for.

Simple quiet moments are etched in my memory and in my heart.

When the wild geese first flew in this fall, weeks ago, they were a noisy, wary, and exciting presence. We couldn't make a move without causing great alarm, not even out of sight up at the house. There was no chance of walking unnoticed around the ponds, no matter how we hid behind the firs, no matter how stealthy we were. One would discover us, then one hundred. Countless wings would flail in panic, sweeping away with them the shrieking wood ducks, the secretive black ducks, the copycat mergansers, all but the oblivious, nearly tame ring neck ducks (which seemed to look at each other amidst the commotion, wonder only for a moment what was happening, and go back to eating).

Finally, I had slipped around to the north alone, circling well back from the water, quietly, carefully, until at last I was hidden in a balsam thicket on the west side of the Big Pond near the new marsh. Grasses and sedges have been filling in the shallows since the Big Dam breached and then swung apart like a gate during a spring wind. Unusually strong, unusually warm, blowing in like a Chinook wind on the prairies, it had melted all of winter overnight. The impact of the windblown ice riding on flood waters had rammed open a twelve-foot gap and lowered the water level in a week-long roar to expose fifteen feet of new shore around the largest pond. I still marvel that the next dam downstream held its ground.

Before I left my hiding place in the thick firs, I watched the skittish geese until I was sure I was undetected. I dropped to my knees and approached, hidden behind an old stump. I waited longer to be sure, then crawled on my elbows into the marsh grasses until I was only just hidden at the water's edge. I moved slowly, I breathed slowly, I thought slowly. Nothing was worth the risk; nothing could match the challenge that moment of sneaking up to this wild, wary, arrogant flock.

Kathy Scott

And there they were. Dozens and dozens of Canada geese, those visiting briefly and their perfect reflections in the black mirror water. Some were wary, on guard. I stayed conscious of not moving. Some were resting, heads curled onto shoulders. Some paddled about; some nibbled green plants rising just above the surface. Some ducked their heads for the green plants below, the reflected goose's cheek-patch rising to meet the one bending down and then blending curiously into one, a two-bodied, headless goose. I stifled the movement of a smile.

The sun showed them off, highlighting their healthy plumage. Several dozed on the sun-soaked beaver lodge; my nest in the grasses was warm. It was a privilege to be there, watching wild geese. Every murmur they made was attenuated and clear. The more I listened, the more I could hear, until I could just make out the soft underlying symphony of ducks and dragonfly wings buzzing and a kingfisher's squawk and splash and a gentle continuous rustle in the dried leaves by my feet, too constant for a mouse, but not so slow as a baby snapping turtle intently focused on the long trek to waters it has never seen.

I redirected my ear, conscious of not moving. What was rustling toward me? It crept like whispers, closer, closer. The geese were undisturbed, it was so quiet, but in my listening world, it was remarkably distinct. At last, a garter snake poked its head through the duff to inspect my knees, decided against the ascent over my legs, and slithered off to round the cape of my toes before continuing its journey. I remember it as if it happened yesterday, not weeks ago.

Changing Planes

I'm thankful for those little things, those frozen moments when the softest whisper becomes a full event, for the dawn just now beginning, darkness turning to blue light, silhouettes of pines and beech appearing out my window. And for David, just arriving, making his coffee, and for Kodiak, now asleep in the chair by my desk. I don't need much else.

But I love my new plane. I admit it.

Yesterday, we drove down to Warren, near the coast, and picked up the Lie-Nielsen low angle block plane with the 45-degree bevel on the blade for optimum cane planing. Although I had talked about having one, I had dismissed the thought immediately as too early in the process. David had simply called ahead to have it waiting on an innocent afternoon drive. Of the two of us, surprising me can be relatively easy.

It is true, I won't actually need a plane for some time. There are a few steps and more than a few hours ahead before my strips are ready. But, like almost everyone, I wanted a plane right away. This one is magnificent, ductile cast iron and shining golden bronze, substantial, exquisitely made, a symbol of the type of rod one hopes to make, of a greater dedication, of a passion for a beautiful craft. I took it apart in the car twice on the way home, and once again on my desk, before carefully wrapping it back in its protective paper for storage in its box, now sitting next to the sheets with the taper dimensions for my rod and the graph of its action. Those things all come later.

I like to muse over things before I jump right in, but I think immersion in cane rodmaking for five or six years, plus helping teach nine others to make rods, attending assorted rodmakers' gatherings for years, reading the rodmakers' list serv daily, collecting or browsing through ten to twenty books... well, enough is enough. It was time to get started.

David and I set up a small workbench by the basement woodstove in the north house. The north house is pretty much devoted to rodmaking, furling leaders, and writing (and sleeping, if you are Kodiak, or surveying your domain from the deck overlooking the ponds). The south house, which we built before the north house came up for sale, is our home, although the plan is to switch that around. The properties are adjacent, so we swallowed hard and found the money to combine them. Some people get rich subdividing; we'll stay poor reuniting.

David clamped the barrel of a heat gun upward on one end of the little portable work bench, then found a vise with an inch-long indentation in one of its opposing jaws and secured it on the other end. That left one entire long face of the small bench free, so he inserted a plastic stopper in one of the pre-made holes along that side. The idea was that I would heat the cane with the heat gun, bend curves straight by arching them against the stopper, and pinch nodes flat with the vise.

This particular bamboo originates from the Tonkin area of China and has been favored in rod construction since the era when H. L. Leonard's daughter brought some home in a Victorian parasol in the seaport town of Bangor, Maine. The Leonard rod shop recognized the superiority of the fibers over the Calcutta cane then in use. Tonkin grows tall, about forty feet in three months, and is dense with power fibers which run its length. To support such tall, straight growth as forty feet, this grass grows (as do most grasses) with nodes, dams across the hollow interior roughly every twelve to eighteen inches, closer together toward the ground where more support is needed, placed farther apart as it reaches the sky.

When it is cut and then divided, the resulting splits have remnants of these nodes which must be filed off, sanded flat, or gouged out, if the eventual strip is to be smooth and uniform. David had started the process before I scavenged these strips, but there were still bumps which would need further attention.

Bamboo culms, the intact sticks of cane, are most often split not sawn into individual strips. Being a natural material, bamboo splits like wood, more or less straight down its length along the grain. For the uniform strips of a fly rod, straight strips are preferable, so rodmakers apply heat and deftly bend each strip's irregularities as straight as possible.

If each strip is six feet long and has, say, three bends per strip and also three nodes, and I picked seven of the eight tip strips to do (six plus one extra) and six butts, I could count on seventy-eight careful heat applications, seventy-eight careful bends or pinches in the vise. More, if pinching created a subsequent bend.

David picked up the first strip and sighted along it. "See the bends?" he asked.

Well, sort of. At least, I could tell that the strip wasn't completely straight. He went on.

"There's an S-curve between these nodes, and a big sweep toward the other end. I go for the big sweeps first, myself, but it's your call. Look to see where the bend actually starts."

I couldn't see it clearly. "Here?" I asked, touching a likely spot.

"Well, close," he said patiently. "It looks like it's there, but that's right at a node. You want to avoid bending the cane at a node if you can. No sense in stressing the nodes any more than you have to. I'd hate to have the strip break."

I thought, I'd hate to have it break, too.

He showed me with his fingers and my eye on the cane, and I could see that the bend really started just after the node.

"Hold it pith side down, low over the heat gun, almost touching it. It's okay if it scorches a little. You may even see some red from single stray fibers burning off. If you keep a little pressure on either side, you might be able to feel when the cane gets more pliable."

I was taking it all in. I'd heard it before, I'd even explained it to others, but hearing it once more was not a bad thing. We pulled on our gloves. David demonstrated heating the sweeping bend, then laid it on the workbench and arched it against the stopper, pulling down gently on either end of the strip.

"Bend the cane by applying pressure on either side of the stopper and holding the strip flat on the workbench with downward pressure at the same time, so it won't twist." He held up the strip, eyed it into the light, then passed it to me. The bend was gone. I tried to find the next bend, putting my finger on my best guess. I was closer that time. After two heat applications and a meek attempt followed by a stronger attempt at reshaping the strip, I had the next bend out.

Then David demonstrated pressing a node.

"Prep work is everything. The more time you spend flattening these bumps by pressing the fibers into line, the less you'll have to plane off later. On a blond rod (bamboo which hasn't been flamed darker), filing off a node doesn't show so much. On a flamed strip like this, filing leaves a lighter mark and gets pretty obvious." He inspected the strip to find a node which needed pinching. "Look at the enamel side, where it's flamed. If there's an obvious bump, heat just that part, just the node, and then put it in the vise with the enamel side toward the smooth jaw and the pith toward the cut out, the indentation. When you squeeze the jaws together, the enamel side will be pushed flat, the displaced bump going into the indentation. You can plane that pith off later."

He demonstrated, and then I looked for another node to try. Some of them were pretty flat already from David's initial preparatory work, filing the nodes with the culm still intact before flaming. The rodmaker's mantra: prep work is everything. The smoother the strip and the straighter, the easier the planing will be.

We worked together on the strip until it seemed to David that we'd done all we could to make it uniform, and I studied it as a standard. Then I laid it apart from the others, over on the flat top surface of the drying oven. One down, six more tip strips to go. David made sure I felt comfortable, then headed upstairs to his bench to finish the initial planing of some of his own tip strips.

Alone with my cane. I chose a new strip at random and sighted along it. Interesting. It started as one strip and split into two. Forked. I lowered and examined it, just to be certain that it was not forked in reality. It wasn't. Then I tried sighting along the strip again. Forked. Hmm. I had succumbed to tired eye muscles only recently, so this was new ground. I closed one eye, and the fork merged into one strip. Glasses are a tool; all tools have to be used appropriately and with some skill. I just had to figure out how to use these in this application.

There were two obvious bends in the strip, but I couldn't see exactly where. I decided to run my hand along the strip until I thought there was a bend, then apply pressure to the strip at that spot while still sighting along it. If the bend came out a little, I had found the spot.

Just before the second node, the strip swept to my left. I applied a little pressure to my right, and the strip appeared straighter. I lowered the strip while still pinching the probable bend, lined that spot up over the heat gun, and then grasped the cane on either side. The gun hummed, and the faint odor of the sweet warm cane came drifting up, like a smudge of native sweet grass, I thought. Nice. I checked the pith twice until it was just a little browned, then levered the strip against the plastic stopper while holding it flat on the workbench. I could just feel the warmth of the cane through my leather gloves. After waiting twenty seconds for it to cool, probably longer than necessary, I sighted along the strip. Straighter. Good.

I repeated the procedure on the next strip, running my hand along it until I found a bend that would correct under pressure, then applying heat, then arching it on the workbench. The heat gun continued to hum and the aroma of sweet grass again began to fill the air. It worked again; the second strip was straighter. I decided to go for a node.

Changing Planes

Between the two bends I had corrected was just a bit of a bump, but one that was obvious and that I could fix. I circled around to the other side of the bench and held the node over the heat gun, checking carefully and often, until the node seemed quite warm. Then I placed the node in the jaws of the vise, pith side toward the indentation, and tightened the jaws together to hold it. With both hands, I tightened the jaws more and looked at the strip. It wasn't responding. Either I needed to reheat it, potentially making it brittle, or I needed to tighten the vise more, potentially cracking the node. I had to decide before it cooled, so I reasoned that I was a weakling and put a foot on the crosspiece between the legs of the workbench and tightened the vise with all my might. The cane conformed, deforming into the indentation. Pretty cool. I was about to release it from the vise when David called down to see how I was doing.

"I'll bring it up in a minute," I promised. He'd already taken a lot of potential planing time helping me; I could just as easily run upstairs now for his insights. I tried to release the vise. Okay, not so easily. Would I actually have to ask David to come down and open the vise for me? I grinned to myself - never! I pushed the vise handle through to the opposite side, push not pull to turn, gathered all my strength and body mass, and hit it hard. Irresistible force driven by irresistible will. The jaws loosened, and I trotted upstairs with the strip.

David paused to sight it toward the light. "Looks pretty good," he observed. "Try it. See anything?"

I took the strip. It was bent. I handed it back.

Kathy Scott

"When you pinch a node, sometimes the displaced material creates a new bend. You can pinch nodes first, or correct the strip afterwards if it bends. Or not. In reality, these bends could all just even out, and you could have a perfectly great rod. Maybe no one could tell; I just think it's better to have good straight strips all along. It's an attention to detail thing. You have to decide where you want to be along the continuum." He smiled reassuringly. It was my call, true, but I had been examining cane rods, maybe hundreds of them over the years, and I knew what I hoped to do.

"Could you show me what you'd do next?" I fished.

He touched a spot and told me that he'd try a bend right there. I pinched the place and headed back downstairs. The heat gun hummed, and the smell of sweet grass drifted about. That strip looked good. I exchanged it for number three and sighted down its length.

By the fourth strip, I was immersed. The woodstove was cheery, the work equally warm and friendly. Still, hours were slipping by. David was binding his tip strips with a light cotton cord, so after that strip I called it a night. Kodiak had surrendered already.

That left three tip strips and six butts for this morning, Thanksgiving. Somehow, the holiday seems appropriate. So much of what I'm thankful for seems a part of working those strips, David, our life together, friends, our ethics and values, surprises and working together, the joy in embracing the simple things of life. Not a bad reason for being awake half the night, replaying the past few days in my head while trying to impose some kind of calm, then getting up early. I may not be watching parades on television this year, but the childlike excitement is familiar. I am making my own split bamboo fly rod, not just helping this time. The joy of it makes it hard to focus, but I do. David is sharpening his plane, Kodiak has resumed sleeping by the woodstove, and I'm about to start warming up the heat gun and begin the fifth strip. I'll straighten until it's time for dinner.

Monday, December 1st

The peace that comes with working each cane strip still fills the north house, where Kodiak and I are alone today with the happy ghosts of the weekend's efforts. David drove off to work after first calling some of my colleagues, relaying my predicament, and suggesting substitute plans. At some point during Friday I lost my voice. Cane dust? November cold? It has been three and a half days to this point, and I'll return to work tomorrow, silent or not. Although being unable to speak is more of a handicap in a library than might be imagined, it is still probably less of a nuisance in a school's library media center than in the classroom.

At least for today, though, it's rest for my throat. I caught up silently on life's neglected details, bills, and correspondence, until Kodiak could contain himself no longer. Why was I home if we weren't going to do something? We made a brief sidetrack to the mailbox with all of the letters, raised the little red flag on the side in the mail carrier's line of sight, then dropped down the hill out of the clearing toward the pond.

Kathy Scott

Each walk around the chain of ponds is very much like the work on each strip of cane. There are details to notice, dams to inspect, new tracks in the soft adjacent paths, a moose scrape here, a wind-felled balsam fir there. There is also time to be lost in thought, embracing the moment and embracing the past, looking forward to the future.

A strong wind followed last night's rain and flurries, surrounding me in the December music of spruce and fir, of crackling old pine boughs. The air felt fresh and alive, and I felt wonderful, silent or not. At the Grass Dam, the sweet old beaver swam so curiously close that the slap of its tail showered my raingear with spray. Glad I wore it. We see each other so often, I wonder if this beaver might become so accustomed to us that I'll be able to touch it. We gave up long ago on keeping it wild - our very presence makes that impossible.

Before Kodiak lead me to Hemlock Ridge, I was wet again, rain. The sun pushed through the cloudburst quickly and lit the marsh grasses a golden brown all across to Bull Moose Cove. The water sparkled, dancing with sun rays, and the barren flooded trees rising up through the waves were bathed in silver gray. But by the time we jumped the stream and made that last turn back toward the house, darkened clouds had overpowered the sunlight and were building taller in the wind. As we emerged from the rocking trees, sleet stung my face and then it was gone. A moody, exciting day.

Those last three strips had relaxed easily in the warmth of the heat gun Thanksgiving morning, and we had gained time for walking Kodiak like this before the Big Dinner. David's sister, Barbara, our near neighbor to the north, had invited a small crowd ranging from us to neighborhood strays to friends who were like family. There had been two puppies for Kodiak to puzzle over, a beagle (world's cutest puppies) and a Schnauzer, while our happy jumble of humanity shared laughter and stories and who'd seen what movies and good food, mashed potatoes, green beans, cranberry stuff, pumpkin stuff, and the most perfect turkey ever served. Afterwards, the desserts were too good and too rare a treat to bypass no matter how full we all were. It all carried us well into the evening, until we were back working with our cane.

David had planed by the main wood stove, shaving Hutch's butt strips to the final dimensions of a Payne 101 taper. I'd returned to my strips in the basement. I would run up the stairs to have him check each one, examining it for bends I'd missed, teaching me to develop my eye for straightening bamboo, and he'd come down to stoke the fire, a quick break, a chance to share a thought or two. Kodiak had taken turns up and down, sleeping at our feet. He was such an active puppy, a lively husky-cross, that we had always wondered if he'd ever mature to napping at our feet. He was so very lively as a puppy, we occasionally wondered if he'd live to be an older dog. At ten, he's a model friend. It's hard to imagine life without him.

The following morning, my six butt strips had been far more stubborn than the tip strips had been. A less cooperative culm, no doubt. I had to remind myself that what effort I may have saved by using David's leftover splits could be a false savings. After all, my jump start was in using not just leftover strips, but rejected strips. Three of the six were absolute snakes.

Kathy Scott

Once the heat gun started humming, the cane had shaped itself to my wishes, a bend here, back a bit there, a long sweep down between those nodes. Time suspended and I was immersed in the craft of it again, the sweet smells, the warmth, awe as each strip straightened more and more and then lay flat. Finally the details had become second nature, as if this was just what I did, internalized, leaving me free to muse over other things. Only afterwards did I do the math: forty minutes a strip.

David had wound string around his butt strips, forming them into a hexagonal blank, and suspended them from the top of the door frame near his bench. He'd helped me gather my strips and secure them together. I'd tucked them up on a rafter for safekeeping. Then we'd settled in near Kodiak and shared the woodstove for a while. Our talk of bamboo and the stuff of life had settled on a neighbor just a few miles up the road, but a century away.

Only twenty-odd miles north then west, there had once been a working bamboo rod shop. Charles Wheeler was the son of a Farmington gunsmith during a boom for that profession, the Civil War. After the States reunited, young soldiers returned to tell their brides in Maine of lands in the Midwest more suitable for farming than these rocky soils, and the fields and the gunsmiths were both in danger of being left behind. But other Civil War veterans had both retirement pensions and experience camping. They traveled to Maine's pristine lakes to test the wartime fishing stories of their Maine counterparts and found those lakes full of trout. With the extension of the narrow gauge railroad from Farmington up to the heart of the Rangeley Lakes, a new tourism emerged to replace the old economy, urged along by the pen of Cornelia "Fly Rod" Crosby and the entrepreneurs who built sporting camps and large hotels in the area.

It didn't take much to persuade Charles Wheeler to make something new, a split cane fly rod patterned after one presented by an out-of-state angler, then improved upon. The time of the gunsmith was past; he needed to adapt. By the Centennial Celebration of the reunited nation in 1876, the six-sided Wheeler fly rod had gained such notice that it was awarded an exposition medal. Over five thousand were produced in a two-story wooden building which still stands on Broadway in Farmington, not far from the music hall (now a store) where Charles Wheeler conducted the band that was to bear his name for many years. He used a bamboo director's baton. In his rodmaking shop, he employed up to fourteen men who would have split and straightened the cane and converted the strips into the six triangles necessary to craft six-sided blanks. To do that, they relied at least in part on a secret beveling machine to shape and taper those strips, and my next step would be somewhat the same.

The raw strips split out of the culm are more or less straight edged. As the holiday weekend progressed, we pulled each of mine through a 90-degree edge trimming cutter, just to be sure. To continue, however, the strips have to be equilateral triangles, 60-degree angles - six triangles joined together to form a hexagon, like a pencil and like a bamboo fly rod.

While I could place each strip in a form and use a hand plane to achieve the 90-degree angle on each side of my triangle, I'd already abandoned the purists' path when I adopted David's discarded strips instead of splitting out my own. I was in this purely for the joy of it, and therefore allowed to choose my own place along the continuum of handmade purity. I decided to power bevel the 60-degree angles. There would still be plenty of hand planing to follow.

David laid aside his own strips to show me the way. He had to readjust his planing form to the measurements needed for Sean's Payne 100, a good pausing point. Although I'd assisted with the rough beveling several times here at home and during classes, I welcomed the chance to work together and to learn with a more invested eye.

This particular beveller was made by California craftsman Jerry Wall. Basically, it's a smooth, off-white metal box about 12" by 18" by 6" thick with a rotating bit protruding from one side directly over a slot in a wooden guide protected by a Plexiglas shield. The cane strip would be fed into one end of the slot toward the cutter. A small mechanical arm holds it down and in place, and another keeps it down as it is being fed along the slot toward the other end.

David looked my first tip strip over.

"Looks good," he said, eyeing the straightness and examining the smoothness of the nodes. "I'll feed the narrower end in first. Let's keep the enamel side tight against the inside edge of the slot. We'll make a nice constant feed through."

I nodded and, at his signal, switched on the attached shop vac. He tested the strip in the slot first, noting that the cutting edge just touched it, then retracted the strip, turned on the beveller, and fed the strip in. It augmented the roar of the shop vac to a pitch that only the scream of the cutter biting cane could overcome. We used hand signals and wore ear protectors. I had pulled the cane through and handed it back to David oriented exactly as it had emerged. He had examined it, decided to bevel the same side a bit more, and fed it in again. When I handed it back to him, he flipped off the beveller's power switch, and I turned off the shop vac.

"Look at the end," he said, showing it to me. "We have a nice 60-degree angle started on this edge."

I knew we wouldn't be beveling on the enamel side of the strip where the power fibers that run through the cane are concentrated, the edge that was flamed brown. When I noticed that the identification marks on the strip were disappearing, beveled away, I stopped to align the strip with the other tip strips. A thick mark from a blue felt tip pen ran diagonally across them near one end. When matched, they indicated the place order of each strip in the original culm of cane.

I rotated each strip in turn and drew blue hash marks on one facet instead, tiny lines- first one line on the first strip, then two on the second, three on the third. On the forth, I skipped a space and began a second set of hash marks, three tiny lines, a space, one more. Many rodmakers have adopted the three-mark groupings to indicate the order of the strips, and a little thrill ran through me as I realized that I was marking my own.

Kathy Scott

We switched positions and urged the machines back to life. I fed the strips through until the tip strips satisfied us both, we took a break, and then we went ahead with the butt strips. These had more of my preparation effort invested, and I hoped David would find them acceptable. He looked them over.

"These are better strips. Must have been a better culm," he grinned. Maybe. He also knew how much time I had taken with them; initially they'd been snakes. He could also have been lying to make me feel better. I chose to go with the first thought - they were better strips. They certainly fed through the beveller smoothly. We were finished with all six before we were ready for leftover turkey sandwiches.

David wondered if we might experiment with a slight run on the enamel side, if I didn't mind. The enamel on the culm is quite rounded and must be flattened in the course of crafting the rod, one way or another. Otherwise, all of the planing is done on the other two facets. One slight pass could begin the leveling process nicely, giving me a starting base. I thought we might as well try it on this rod as any, and nodded my agreement.

We passed each strip through the beveller again, this time just occasionally touching the surface. The toasted brown gave way to a more tortoise shell mottle, and it felt smoother, flatter. I liked it.

"It'll be fine," David said. "Now we should bind these together so that they don't warp or bend as they continue drying. You could even select which six of those seven tip strips you're keeping, and we could bind them on a M-D fixture." M-D, Martin-Darrell, about to become another person helping me in the making of this rod, had passed a long, shadowy evening with us on the front porch of a log cabin on the Yellowstone. His fixtures were a length of aluminum extruded to look like a six-line star in the cross-section. A strip is laid in each resulting V, then wrapped with the others in place, mimicking the way they would fit together as a blank but held tight and therefore straight while waiting or being heat treated.

I could have chosen my final strips, true, but I was hungry and Kodiak was ready for a walk. I bunched the strips together instead and secured the blue-marked strips with a series of blue rubber bands, the red-marked butt strips with red bands, and put them on the rafter to dry.

It wasn't until later, on our walk around the ponds, that I had realized something remarkable. We had crossed the Grass Dam, ascended the ridge as far as the Duck Cove cutoff, and approached the water, when David pointed out one of those details that makes life special. A late season V of geese was approaching from the North. He'd heard them first, and we watched the gray sky until they appeared just above the tree line. Over the silver water, their necks bent down and sideways, they evaluated the resting potential of our ponds. Then their wingspreads changed as they came braking in, losing altitude rapidly until they were skiing on the water. We held hands as we watched, hidden behind some balsam fir.

But the remarkable part was this: We had had a wonderful three days together and I hadn't been able to speak a word. Not a bit of voice since Friday, the day after Thanksgiving. I could have ventured a whisper, maybe, but since that extended recovery time, I didn't. For three days we'd been working and walking

Kathy Scott

together, one of us silent. It reminded me of watching the movie Edward Scissorhands without headphones on a long flight home. The movie was so intuitively understandable that we'd both forgotten we'd never heard the words until we saw it a year later on television.

It may be tough to discuss philosophy with a mute partner, but it's not hard to live it. Only ten more minutes, and David will be home from work again. I'll bet he brings pizza.

Changing Planes

Nobody knows what will happen, what catastrophes,
what miraculous transformations. In order to maintain faith,
to plan for the future, the world must be simplified.

Here is the window out of which you can see a tree,
a bright red flower, green grass extending over the hill.

~ Louis Jenkins

Changing Planes

Saturday, December 6th
Winter Storm Warning

Instead of a classic New England white Christmas, so far the season had only been able to muster a return to near zero temperatures and star-filled, snowless nights. Days had been accented with the brown toned highlights and shadows of low-angle sunlight. Our road was more like the cold dusty Tibetan plateau than a snow-covered lane for a horse drawn sleigh. At least we'd avoided long hours of shoveling and snowblowing at the most hectic time of the year.

That was about to change.

With a long and well-branched list of things to do, we were a bit chagrined to have the weekend forecast turn into a winter storm warning and blizzard watch. So much for a weekend to chip away at the list. We ran to town early for dog food, a few groceries, and gas for the snow blower. Then, David dropped Kodiak and me off at the north house - shop - with half the goods and drove to the south house with the other half. He was going to move the snow blower from the storage shed to the back door and prep it for the Big Event.

"Expect a foot," they cautioned on the news, "but it could be two."

Kathy Scott

I pulled the little green wagon to the edge of the woods to gather fallen pine branches for dry kindling, and Kodes came along. He waited patiently, as ten-year-old dogs do, while I snapped branches into stove-lengths and piled them in. Still, I took pity on him and slipped him out of his leash. The pond just below us looked more like an ice rink than a beaver bog, smooth snow-free surface potentially hiding weak spots that wouldn't support his weight; we'd been down that road twice, barely salvaging happy endings. But I reasoned that he'd stay with me, the pond being down the hill and the mice trails being right at our feet. It had been near zero all week, so the ice would most likely support a sixty-five pound dog, anyway. It would probably support a couple of ice skaters, too, if they didn't have to get ready for a major snowstorm. We'd waited all fall for the chance, a slim chance always, to skate on ice like this, wild rink-like ice, ice ringed with spruce and balsam fir, an exhilarating landscape with ice so smooth we could look up from our feet to see it without fear of rough spots or ice skate-eating pressure cracks.

Oh, well. Not going to happen.

I pined for wild skating while I picked up boughs for kindling, and Kodiak nosed about. The branches cracked and snapped with little effort in the cold. The pond had been singing with cold all week, long whomps in the night, songs of winter as sure as loons sing songs of summer. Maybe there were pressure cracks, anyway. I was lost in dreams of ice and the raven like joy of soaring across great distances effortlessly, the closest thing to flying I can do.

Then Kodiak's bark broke through my thoughts.

Changing Planes

A second of fear gripped me, but there he was, just feet away, safe. He was barking toward the ice below, toward the divided beaver dam, the two ends stretching from the shores but not quite touching, the jetties. I looked just in time to see two bucks leap from the east jetty. The leader landed on the ice half way across, leaped again, up and on to the west jetty, and bounded off. The second buck, though, suddenly lost its footing midway as the ice gave away. It disappeared into the black water.

My heart nearly stopped; then the deer resurfaced, flailing.

Kodiak barked wildly as the deer struggled for front-feet purchase, but the thin layer broke away. The poor creature just gained a hoof hold and pulled its shoulders out only to have its chances break apart. It sank back under the cold black water. Again. Then again.

I punched the button of the two-way radio.

"David! David! Are you there?" I left the anxiety in my voice so he'd know something was urgent.

"I'm right here. What's happened?" his voice replied.

"A deer fell though the ice between the jetties of the old dam and can't get out!"

"What can we do?" he asked, a good question.

"I don't know, but if you bring the ice-climbing rope we can figure out if there's any way to help it." We'd switched from attempting vertical climbs in Maine's mountains to carrying the rope in our rescue kit the first time Kodiak broke through the ice.

Kathy Scott

Then I realized we had a bigger problem. In the short length of our conversation, Kodiak had bounded down the hill. I called out to stop him, but he had another calling, obviously. Well, great. The deer, still struggling, needed help, the commotion luring Kodiak closer, but if I followed, Kodes would gain more confidence. He could head right out on the ice and go through. I waited, helpless, high up the hill, while Kodiak approached the shore. To my relief, his distance comfort zone ran out, and he stopped there to persuade me to follow.

"No way, Kodiak," I called down. "You come back up here! Come here!" I tried my most serious voice. "Kodiak, come here!"

Deaf ears.

Kodiak, even more frustrated, resumed telling off the trespassing deer, stamping his front feet to drive the point home. The deer was growing tired and maybe hypothermic. It had settled down into the cold water with only its head out, maybe resting, maybe played out, but quiet enough to suddenly notice a maniac dog. It seemed immediately pumped with adrenaline and spun around to the opposite direction, away from this new danger. It struggled again, facing the other way, hooves again gaining access to the ice, shoulders straining upward, urged on by the trespasser-evictor of all time. Finally, it was out, up on the ice, bounding onto the west jetty and disappearing into the firs on the heels of its distant companion.

Kodiak paused mid-stomp, woofed once, and turned to sprint up to me, grinning.

Amazing.

Changing Planes

I hugged him and roughed him up while I radioed David - All over, headed your way with Kodiak, to be known hereafter as "our hero."

I'd lost all urge to go ice skating and thought I'd enjoy working on the snow blower and hauling a little firewood instead.

We stocked the woodpiles at both houses, made cheery fires, and just beat the arrival of the evening's storm. By five, the workshop was cozy, snow swirling in the darkness outside but David planing Sean's butt strips and Kodiak napping by the woodstove inside. I ventured out to retrieve holiday cards to address from the south house and pushed the snow off all of the decks to gauge the accumulation, three inches and just getting started. David clears the driveways when the snow depth is four or five inches. The evening settled into a shopwork-snowwork routine, apparently to continue throughout the weekend; maybe there will be wild ice skating next year.

Next year. Not that far off on the calendar, where December seems full of additional ink. As a concession to the season and the knowledge that I could not give them anything approaching my full attention, I decided to mark my strips beyond all chance of mistakes, then retire them. Reluctantly.

I pulled them down from the rafters and laid them in order on the workbench. Then I made a little drawing similar to the drawings David always makes to scrutinize the nodes and the possibilities for alignment. I marked the desired temporary and finished lengths I would need for this particular rod, now firmly in my mind as modeled after the Garrison 193. By drawing arrows, I chose a three-three stagger, aligning every other node

Kathy Scott

around the rod, three half way between the other three. It's an easy stagger to arrange. Since nodes change the material properties of the cane, a balanced stagger, whatever pattern, lends toward the uniform response of the whole rod. I checked to make sure that none of the nodes would lie too close to the tip or to a ferrule in the finished rod; I don't need any potential weak spots there.

    The eventual rod will be six feet nine inches, eighty-one total inches, so each matched half with hardware will be forty and a half inches. In case of problems, I left them three inches too long for the time being, cutting the strips evenly with a small, fine-toothed saw. The tips I left longer than the butts, partly because there was cane to spare and partly to help me tell them apart should the colors disappear in planing. The butt ends of the tips I colored blue and the butt ends of the butts red. How to remember that easily? Blue sky, up, tips, and red? Dirt? An imperfect analogy, but it seemed to work for me. I tucked all of the bundled strips up on a beam to wait for me. Maybe I could get back to them yet this coming week.

Changing Planes

Saturday, December 13th

Some weeks are snowier than others. This past week set new standards right from the start.

We monitored that storm last Saturday night until David let Kodiak out one final time and checked the accumulation. Still just eight inches, significant snow yes, catastrophic proportions, no. This is why David was almost irritated when Kodiak whined at 3 am.

"Man, Kodes," he grumbled, "you just went out four hours ago!"

He found the door and the end of the snap-lead he'd left tailing inside, attached Kodiak, and was not pleased when Kodiak refused to go out into the storm.

"It's just snow," I heard him say. "You went out in it earlier."

Kodiak was balking and I was waking up. What was that noise? David was still persuading Kodiak when a semiconscious realization shot through me. On full alert, I recognized the start-stop sound, the smell of kerosene.

"Is that the furnace?" I asked.

We both listened to the clues drifting up the stairs. It was the furnace. David scrambled downstairs to look and I dressed on the way down the stairs behind him. I opened the walk-out basement door for ventilation as he peered into the stove, our improvised division of labor. David would attend to the mechanical end and air out the place, Kodiak supervising, while I pulled on the last of my gear, switched on the high beam of the headlamp, and plunged into the blizzard to check the exhaust pipe.

A real Nor'easter. The storm was held out to sea by high pressure which had stalled it just long enough to pick up plenty of moisture, carry it counterclockwise north into the cold and on down to us, heavy snow and wind from the Northeast. It was already well over my knees, drifts approaching my waist and blocking my path.

I needed to check the combination exit/intake pipe under the north eve, but the shortest route lay under the deepest snow. With a shovel as a walking support, I tried circling the house toward the south, instead, slowly plowing through to the east decks. The danger of these situations became pretty obvious. Like prairie ranchers who run a rope from the house to the barn, I needed some clue where to go. The blizzard was blinding and dense. I kept one hand on the house, knowing that a step away could translate into a tough time.

My headlamp finally lit the bank that used to be the decks, and I struggled over and past them to the north side. We had built the house for the maximum efficiency and lowest cost we could manage, essentially achieving the insulation of an earthberm by sinking the first floor of a small cape into the ground as a basement, the peaked roof appearing as an A-frame. While wonderfully efficient to heat or to cool, this resulted in eaves only three feet above the level of the ground.

Trouble. On the north side, there was no longer a distinguishable line between the roof and solid ground, just one long slope. I guessed the spot where the exhaust might be, flipped the shovel blade backward to slice a clean downward cut, and pulled loose a foot of snow, the lower edge sooty. A second try revealed the stifled exhaust.

I wallowed around to the nearest basement window, dug down to find it, and tried unsuccessfully to signal David that he could proceed with the mechanical end. I could see through the window that the walk-out door was still open so the air inside would be safe. I decided to use my energy to shovel and go back in to tell him afterwards.

The snow was light and elusive, the wind was howling. It was invigorating work, even at three in the morning. Kodiak the Hero, I thought, first the deer, then us, all in twenty-four hours. I fell into a rhythm throwing snow high and into the darkness to the north, creating a clear area extending out about three feet from the foundation below the exhaust. I turned west and cleared a small path until I'd made my way back to the door.

We guessed that we could wait until morning to go out again, that it would be smarter in the long run to get some sleep, but we dozed lightly. We were both awake enough an hour later to hear the furnace sputter again. The smell of exhaust crept up the stairs and met us on the way down. Once we managed to open the door, I measured the snow depth. Sheltered from the wind, twenty-three inches and still coming down.

Kathy Scott

We stayed up after that, passing time by discussing modifications to the exhaust vent. We spent the next day watching the storm wind down from behind the shovel and snow blower. David was thrown about as the snow blower tried its best, the big, heavy, no-storm-can-beat-me snow blower. It tunneled under the snow. He'd replaced its shear bolt with our last and was crossing his fingers when I went out to find the mailbox.

One thing about Maine, the roads do get plowed and in a timely fashion. As near as I could tell, the berm in front of our mailbox made it six feet from the new edge of the road and was taller than the mailbox. I scaled the bank and traversed to the box's assumed position, rolling boulder sized snowballs away with both hands and some shoulder work. After an hour, I had vacated a nice area in front of the mailbox which would give it some credibility, a courtesy to our neighbors Scott and Donnie. That it was unscathed in such a blinding storm is a tribute to Scott and Donnie's ability with their contracted snowplow. By then, my tired hands could no longer grip my shovel. It was 3 pm.

David had freed only the north ends of the drives at each house but came in at my request and passed out on the couch. He freed the ends again just before bedtime after the next pass of the snowplows. The roads and a narrow slot to the truck were clear; we'd make it to work.

We tried it again Monday night. Neither of us needed headlamps in the full moonlight, as calm and bright and beautiful an evening as we could remember. David left work at 9 am on Tuesday when we heard the forecast for pouring rain, maybe by Thursday, followed by falling temperatures. Any remaining snow in the wrong place would turn to snowcrete.

Changing Planes

Supplied with a bag of shear bolts, he tackled the south ends of both drives, trying to dent the six foot plow berms across the end. A long day didn't do it, so he called in reinforcements, neighbors Dave and Dave who can cowboy their four-wheel-drive through any snow bank. They burst through the ends late Wednesday night and freed the mailbox to boot.

Thursday, it rained. It poured all evening. The rivers jammed and overflowed. The student parking lot in Farmington flooded thirty-nine cars. On Friday, the temperature plummeted.

Today under a seamless blue sky and warm, low-angle sunlight, the snow of last weekend consolidated into a good base. We donned short snowshoes and headed north, Kodiak bounding ahead then resting by following in our trail. We stopped at the brook, still flowing at flood level, a beautiful black ribbon between unspoiled white snow banks. Unable to cross, we followed along downstream instead, marveling at otter tracks and a peaceful beauty which seemed more like early March.

While I addressed the delayed cards for the holidays, David planed Hutch's tips, just a strip or two, to .020 oversize, the last step before the final planing. Kodiak napped between us, near the woodstove. I furled a few leaders, satisfying, perfectly twined, little tapered ropes. I considered working with my strips, but there is a foot of snow in the immediate forecast and another storm predicted for Wednesday.

Kathy Scott

Thursday, February 5th

I just started timing the oven: ten minutes at 350 degrees, rotate strips end to end, ten minutes more at 350 degrees. It has been awhile since I worked on my rod, and it feels good to be back to it. Since I laid the bound strips up on the rafter to wait, I've made one hundred furled leaders, we went home for the holidays, and we demonstrated cane rodmaking and furling leaders at the wonderfully friendly fly-fishing show our friend Jim Krul has put together in Connecticut. There, while we were talking in the aisle, someone slipped by to examine one of David's rods. David asked the man's back if he was interested in cane. He turned to reply.

"Some," he said, introducing himself. "I'm Hoagy Carmichael."

"In that case," David recovered quickly, "do you have any advice for me?"

Hoagy Bix Carmichael, who had detailed Everett Garrison's methods and tapers in *A Master's Guide to Building A Bamboo Fly Rod* (what many rodmakers reverently call "The Book"), picked up one of David's split cane fly rods, looked it over, and replied with his characteristic grace, "No, I think you're doing just fine."

Changing Planes

While meeting Hoagy was fun, I wish I'd have said one thing more. I'd like to thank Hoagy Carmichael for his part in writing it all down, for being a part of my life now, too; Everett Garrison developed the taper for this little rod cooking away next to me.

Not really cooking but rather heat treating, driving the remnant moisture out of the strips. The oven is a six-foot long sheet metal box designed by Wayne Cattanach and built by Brett Reiter. The cover pulls off one end to reveal a horizontal metal screen shelf dividing the interior and the long heating elements, mica strips. The temperature control box and thermostat sit on top.

6:52 David came down and pulled the end cover off for me, as I had done many times for him. I donned the leather welding gloves. They were too big and fairly clumsy, but I could just grasp the ends of the M-D fixtures and pull out my bound, steaming strips. The fragrance of sweet grass, sweet cane, drifted around us.

"Good," David said, "it's steaming."

Kathy Scott

I slid both fixtures out, rotated them, then fed the bound strips back into the heat. David replaced the cover while I dialed down the control to hear the click. 325 degrees. Lost a bit of heat.

"That doesn't matter," David explained. "It's not as crucial as when you started. Go ahead, you can begin timing."

I reset the dial higher again. At 6:58, the control clicked at 350 degrees. David stoked the woodstove, checked to see if I was all set, and climbed back upstairs to plane Hutch's last tip strips while I settled in to wait. Six minutes to go.

After Connecticut, there was teaching about rodmaking at a fly fishing show near Boston. Then, just Saturday, we were immersed in a mini-conclave of extended internet friends, the sole purpose to give anglers a chance for hands-on experiences with split cane rods. SuperBoo, the named coined by our Trout Unlimited friend Dave Hedrick as a play on its close proximity to the Super Bowl and a useful mnemonic for remembering the date. Since it's held at our school, Hutch handled the facilities during the event, lines caught in basketball hoops, locked doors. David fielded the cane questions himself or distributed them to fellow rodmakers, seven in attendance. I planned the event, coordinated, and played host, making introductions, anticipating needs, pointing in the right directions. Nearly one hundred anglers attended with as many bamboo fly rods, Garrison tapers, F. E. Thomas, Payne, Dickerson, more. T-shirt sales and raffles add to the entertainment and support the high school fly fishing club Hutch and I coach. Good fun, good events, good reasons for not getting back to my rod.

Time is always a consideration.

7:04 I pulled the big gloves back on, turned off the oven and unplugged it. Then I pulled off the end cover and set it on the floor, and finally pulled out the two fixtures, my strips bound to them, my rod. I carried the warm strips upstairs, passing David on the phone. I feigned cleansing myself with the aroma of hot cane. He grinned. Then I leaned my strips against the hearth to cool.

Kathy Scott

Saturday, February 7th

Snow fell most of last night and into this morning, only about six inches so far. We let it lay as a buffer until the afternoon didn't warm to sleet or rain as predicted; then David fired up the snow blower, and I picked up the shovel. Afterwards, we shopped in town for some Valentines before gluing up the butts of both Hutch's Payne 101 and Sean's Payne 100. I walked with Kodiak around the ponds, laying a new snowshoe trail, a snowshoe float, then furled leaders to replenish my stock and relax.

Some anglers tie flies on these winter evenings; a few make split cane fly rods. Mostly, I make fishing leaders, peaceful, restful, contemplative. At a cane rodmakers' gathering years ago, George Barnes and George Rainville had demonstrated the process, a simple adaptation rodmaker Tom Smithwick had improvised from an old, nearly forgotten technique. It's not unlike the process for making rope, once a common craft to supply the ships on the coast of Maine. Centuries ago in England, fourteen-foot tapered lines, a leader and line combination, were made by furling horsetail hair. The fact that furled fly fishing leaders have endured and are enjoying a renaissance as a grassroots art makes them kin, maybe cousins, to the perseverant cane rod.

Changing Planes

Using the new method, a single thread is strung on a board. Pegs are strategically placed so that the visual effect is of making two legs of two loops of thread. The loops are staggered, offset leg to leg, to make a taper. When the legs are spun independently until they are ten per cent shorter, roughly, then hung together while weighted at one end, the two legs intertwine, or furl. The resulting leader is really a five-foot long leader-butt, ready for about four feet of 5X tippet. I was immediately smitten when I found they were memory free and amazingly supple when cast; I need all the help with presentation I can get. Later, our friend Mike Holt taught me to tuck one end-loop back through the freshly constructed leader, then to thread the opposite end-loop through the original end-loop. Pulling the entire leader through leaves a new furled end-loop, just the trick to make changing the tippet easy in swarms of black flies.

George Barnes, George Rainsville, Tom, and Mike assured me they would be pleased if I passed the technique along to the greater community of fly anglers; they had rods to make, other things to do, so I demonstrated furling leaders at gatherings, in fly shops, and on tailgates for a while. Then, David and I filmed all one crisp fall Saturday, and I edited for hours to document the process for even wider sharing. I always give them credit; it's important to remember one's roots. With a boost from the virtual community of the FlyAnglersOnline.com bulletin board, the word spread. It's been great fun meeting people around the world and learning from them the infinite variations and adaptations possible when people work together.

I'm anxious to plane, but right now the leaders and Kodiak come first. Gluing with David was a nice review.

Thursday, March 4

As soon as I decided that I'd make my own split cane fly rod, I wanted a plane. It appears to be a common and normal reaction. It's understandable, I think, at the very least. A hand plane is a woodworking piece of art, object d'art in itself. With its smooth bronze shining deep reflections, its graceful lines and sturdy machined elegance there is no truer symbol of the craft. For a rodmaker there is no tool more useful, none more desirable.

Fortunately, notable artisans who cast and create these planes live between our home at the edge of the North Woods and the rocky coast of Maine, only an hour away. Lie-Neilsen planes have won a place as a standard on the benches of many cane rodmakers with their attention to detail, right down to incorporating a groove to accommodate those who shave bamboo on steel planing forms but wish to avoid shaving the form as well. Ron Barch, who taught David to make his first rod, made each of us a bamboo storage box for Christmas. Inside my plane waited, idle for weeks.

Changing Planes

Mine is an adjustable mouth block plane, the version with a low angle so I can approach getting my hand over it. The model is 60 1/2, named after the old Stanley number of its predecessor. I chose one with the groove. David asked the shop to bevel the blade such that the 12 1/2 degree angle and their secondary hone of about 45 degrees would give a steep angle of 57 1/2 degrees. Planes used for bamboo as opposed to woodworking are often re-beveled, usually aiming toward 55 degrees. With the slightly steeper angle I'd be less likely to tear out the nodes, less likely to have eventual glue lines at the nodes in the finished rod. I left it to his discretion - too early for me to know what I'd prefer. His reasoning sounded good.

By the third weekend in February, it seemed like all things necessary could be put on hold, and David and I placed a planing platform he'd built next to my furling board, then spanning two sawhorses in my corner near the woodstove. I pushed my furling board to the back and repositioned my light to direct the beam on the new work surface. We placed a planing form there, long cold steel, and reviewed my taper. We decided where the strips should lay along the form, and I marked the end limits with masking tape. Then I ran masking tape on the bench top along the length of the planing form and labeled the taper dimensions at five-inch intervals, using a red marker. Butt dimensions, red. I divided those dimensions by two, since each strip extends only half way through the rod, and wrote the second set of labels just above the first. With any luck, I'd align the right strips in the right place and plane them to the correct dimension.

I know rodmakers who say they love planing, that it is restful, that it gives them an intimate sense of contact with the bamboo. My plane and I took a bit to warm up to each other. Despite the low angle, my hand could barely fit over the plane, instead allowing it to rock side to side since my fingers didn't reach far enough to guide along the planing form. Even though the blade comes sharp enough to use, it took a bit of adjusting (me and the plane) to find the thickness of shaving that I found comfortable.

David added a big clamp to the end of the planing form to secure the strip in place, but it took me both hands to pry it open. I tried all of the ways David patiently mentioned to keep the plane level and moving smoothly, but was disappointed. My digital caliper read that my triangle was drifting out of its original equilateral. David showed me how to plane the side that would bring it back, but my hand still felt awkward.

Maybe it was working the clamp with two hands which inspired me to work the plane with two. By arranging my right hand on the back while pressing my left on the front, the strain seemed to abate. Then, as I marked the strip again so I could maintain the six in their original order from the culm, it dawned on me that I could mark the length of the strip at intervals with the felt marker and have an immediate visual gauge showing how level I was holding the plane. Barring uneven spots like nodes, marks planed evenly should disappear uniformly.

David also suggested that I scrape the flamed enamel side of the strips so that the remnant curve of the culm would be gone. The earlier work we'd done with the powered beveller only nicked the surface. More work now, less later, he reminded me. Lying flatter in the planing form would aid in shaving the two non-enamel sides evenly.

All of the strategies added up, and my plane and I became friends. I marked, planed, and measured all six strips until they began to approach twenty thousandths over the desired taper and then called it good for a first time planing. I was curious to see what might be sore in the morning, fingers, wrists, shoulders? The strips were easily coaxed into a hex for storage, a hint of the blank that would follow.

Saturday, March 6

David whispered that he'd started his coffee brewing and would slip next door just long enough to check the progress of his varnish drying on yesterday's wraps. I could hear him downstairs near the back door, bundling up against the damp cold, and then I heard him pull the door tight as he left. Kodiak stretched out

Kathy Scott

with his head on my arm as a pillow. I reached over him with the other hand and scratched the length of his athletic rib cage. He sighed and stretched out farther, switching to deep breathing, ultimate dog contentment. If he was a cat, he'd have been purring.

I felt the smoothness of his hair and the occasional lumps of an older dog and sighed, too, realizing that moments like these can't go on many more years. How many more? Three? Five? A couple extra for staying in such good shape. Then I smiled to remember that there had been moments in his rowdy younger days, mishaps that had made me believe he'd never last this long. Our own parents probably felt that way.

I scratched slowly under his collar, progressing a little at a time up the base of his neck. He murmured a little to encourage me and began his deep steady breathing again.

Opening my eyes a little, I could just see over Kodiak out the window into the fog. A warm front had crept in across the snow during the night. It lingered now as a heavy mist, softening the edges of the world outside, balsam needles gently dripping. Colors glowed richer for the dampness, deep greens draping the firs and spruces offset by the ghostly white and mottled black of the birches. Ghostlike, chickadees were appearing out of the morning fog in their ever quick approach to the bird feeder.

Foggy inside, too, but time to start the day.

After waking up during breakfast, we ran the errands life often demands but stopped to pick up some 320 grit clog-resistant sandpaper. Once we'd retrieved Kodiak and moved to the north house, I wrapped it over a sanding block. David final-planed Sean's tip, finishing the last two strips, and I sanded some of the enamel off all six of my butt strips, interrupting him to inspect each one. We used his scraper plane to find that flat which appears flat, but isn't. Unfortunately, I put a tear-out in strip number three, a tiny sawtooth in the cane which could splinter. I hoped to fix it by carefully trimming it away as I plane. I'd watched these on past rods in progress; never pull a tear-out; the planing will probably take care of it.

The sanding was a dusty business, so by the time the moon rose above the pines, I'd done enough for one night. What happened to that mental note I'd made to wear a mask when sanding? David quit shortly afterwards, and we sat near the fire on either side of Kodiak on his bed. There was a little growth on his eyelid that didn't seem to bother him much, but we took comfort in having made an appointment with his vet for Monday. We can't help but feel its presence, even when he sleeps.

Sunday, March 7th

We started the day with a few quick chores then decided to treat Kodiak with a brisk walk north of here on the logging roads now deserted during Mud Season. I followed that with a couple of sun-warmed hours with him out on the deck, reading and napping, while David cut Hutch's butt section to length and turned it on a lathe so it would accept the reel seat Hutch had chosen. Kodiak and I kept clear until evening, when I planed three of my butt strips to twenty thousandths of an inch over final size. David guided me through number three, the one with the tear-out. No problem.

Friday, March 12

We walked together with Kodiak before dark. The packed snowshoe float was soft but a trail with enough integrity still to support us without snowshoes. We headed north, the route least likely to tempt Kodiak out on to the graying ice. We weren't sure what the rotting ice would support, and we both felt a bit protective of Kodiak today. His early vet appointment on Monday had started well, the little benign growth easily removed from his eyelid and a shot of antibiotic. But the vet's technician had noticed a swelling where the injection took place, and one visit had lead to another, then another. He started medication today for low blood platelets, ten per cent of what a dog should have.

Ten percent. What does that mean? Neither of us had a clue.

It was reassuring to watch him bound along the bunny trails, leaping the brook where it flowed from the beaver dam. He certainly didn't look ill.

In between his appointments, we spent some time planning for the weekend, as if organizing our time could give us more. That rarely works out, but it seemed worth a try. Time seemed all the more precious.

Changing Planes

If I wanted to sand and plane my butt strips, David would glue. If not, he'd dip Hutch's blank again. I said that I had no strong feelings about it; I could plane or furl leaders. Making leaders is dust-free enough to do in the same room with spar urethane. But if David glued, he said, he could strip off the binding string in the morning, and we could drive down to pick up a new shipment of bamboo later in the day. We were sharing it with downstate rodmaker Scott Chase, twenty culms each; seeing Scott and his family would be a plus. We'd also have time to put in drying splits in the evening. Maybe that was the best plan. He'd glue, I'd plane.

Tonight, I sanded a reluctant, wayward edge on the enamel side, then remeasured with the caliper to see if I'd worked it back to an equilateral triangle again. David joined me to boost my learning curve and morale. We decided that I should go on, so I worked on planing the fourth, fifth, and sixth butt strips, never quite reaching twenty thousandths over but approaching it at least on all six strips. David says he was pretty conservative at first, too.

Meanwhile, David built the fires, then readied Sean's tip strips for gluing. I paused to pamper Kodiak and to give him his steroids and antibiotics. He preferred uninterrupted napping, so I pulled myself away. David helped me tape my strips together into a hex. I wiggled the taped together butt once or twice for fun, then leaned it in the corner next to the tip strips, still bound on the M-D fixture and looking relatively huge. David suggested that we could bevel them down a bit more mechanically, but I think I need the planing practice. I still draw marks to judge if I'm holding the plane level.

Kathy Scott

After I bagged my cane shavings, David helped me switch the planing form to the back of my bench and bring the furling board forward. While he dips on Sunday, I'll make leaders. I dialed Scott's number to arrange for the cane pickup while David set the two bottles that make epoxy near the woodstove to warm them for gluing. On wax paper on the counter, he had already sanded the apex off each of the strips we were about to glue, leaving a tiny interior channel for the excess epoxy. Scott answered and we solidified plans for the cane pickup; then I gave the phone to David. I stoked the fire and scratched Kode's ears so we'd all be set to glue.

Tuesday, March 16

Sunday was typically mid-March, the weather pausing long enough for me to work more enamel off the tip strips outside. It was sunny and 40 degrees when David carried the planing form out to the deck and laid it on the wide flat top of the railing, a nice work height. There, I'd have full view of the ponds, and Kodiak could plump down on his thick green bed, perched to watch for anything of interest.

I carried out the six tip strips, freed them from their bindings, and aligned them in order on the railing. With the big clamp for gripping each strip on the planing form, a soft brush for cleaning away the debris, a scraping razor blade, sunglasses, warm vest, and tight leather gloves, I was ready.

Changing Planes

For what, again? Almost too nice to concentrate.

David gave me a quick review of the technique and goal: to scrape off the charred enamel and smooth the nodes until the surface was flat. Power fibers could show a bit. Call him if I had questions. He'd be sanding Hutch's dipped blank in preparation for its second coat, then gluing up cork rings in groups of three in preparation for making the grip.

It all came back to me. I retrieved the file and swapped out of my sunglasses. Still forty degrees, but clouding up. March. I selected the first strip and laid it in the planing form, enamel side up, butt end of the strip even with a red mark I'd drawn on the form. It was just an arbitrary oversize spot I'd chosen so I could do all of the strips the same. Measurements for the taper would come farther down the road.

By using both hands plus a leg for leverage, I was able to squeeze open the clamp. Once open, I could hold it with one hand and maneuver the clamp into place over the strip about a foot up from the butt end. I released it slowly, and the clamp secured the strip in place on the form.

There was no breeze so I was pretty confident that the dust from filing wouldn't drift. I decided not to wear a face mask, choosing comfort and fresh air over the chance of a return bout of bamboo induced respiratory distress. Given the setting, it seemed worth a low risk.

Grasping the handle of the file with my right hand and pressing the gloved fingers of my left hand near the file's end helped me to gauge the angle. I laid the file diagonally across the strip and began to remove the enamel in short strokes. I checked the buildup in its teeth; it would need to be cleaned fairly often. I checked the strip. There was a nice swipe of charred enamel missing from the middle of the strip - good!

I started in again, and David came out to check on things about the time I retrieved the wire brush to clean the file. He offered help, so I asked him to double check my work. He showed me that the part I'd done looked nicely flat and the power fibers were just beginning to show, but that there was a dip on either side of the first node. He didn't think that it would hurt to file more off, my call. I'd like my rod to approach his in craftsmanship, so I took his advice.

Kodiak went back in for a turn close to David, and I went back to my filing. I'd only just pronounced the first strip done when they both returned. No rushing. David inspected my strip and agreed that it was done enough for the time being. Kodiak surveyed the ponds then snuggled in to his bed to watch over them, David went off to glue cork rings together, and I started strip number two. Other things were on my mind.

It was a good atmosphere for thinking: fresh air, a slow but satisfying craft, a late winter day that held the promise of spring. A good day for gaining some perspective. It was time to think about time itself, about mortality, about continuance into the future. Some rodmakers see those things in their cane, an enduring presence over time. I feel like I can touch the past sometimes when I pick up a tool used by one of the classic rodmakers or have a chance to cast a classic rod. There's a certain insight into the heart there. My heart had been in a battle with my head all week, and it felt safe to allow the showdown.

Changing Planes

    Lying near me, ever alert, Kodiak looked absolutely fine. He was wide awake and on the ready for a good romp or a chance to defend his world from an encroaching moose. His patience with my rod work I attributed to his good character, acceptance of our habits, and the great view from this high perch. He'd so convinced us of his vitality that we questioned the treatment the vet proposed.

    David and I think of ourselves as reasonably well-informed. I had worked for a medical school for four years when I was in college; osmosis must count for something. So what were we missing? What are platelets and how are they lost? Why do dogs need them, and what if Kodes really only had ten percent of his? A few phone calls and some Internet sites told us that platelets repair blood vessel walls and help clotting, among other things, and that their numbers can diminish if the bone marrow doesn't produce enough or if they are used up somehow.

    While I dialed my dad and waited those amazingly brief moments for the connection to travel one thousand miles, I counted myself lucky that, so far, I hadn't found all those miles between me and an urgent visit. I'll always be thankful that I grew up on a working farm, that I spent summer days raking hay in one field while I watched my Dad baling hay in the next, winter days in the hay loft throwing down bales he fed to the young cattle. Once an aging Hereford cow had needed a wound cleaned daily and an accompanying shot, and Dad taught me to do it. He confined her to a big corral so David and I would herd her into the stanchion at one end. I'd note any changes in the vet's drain in the tumor on the side of her head and then spray it thoroughly with disinfectant. I'd remove the hypodermic syringe

Kathy Scott

from its box, insert the needle through the thin skin-like membrane on the antibiotic bottle, and pull it full. Dad had shown me how to step out of the cow's peripheral view, make a quick dart of the needle into her hip, and depress the plunger before she even realized the prick. What vet work Dad doesn't do, he assists. Platelets were a new problem, though, so he consulted the Merck manual for us, but it was his voice that gave me the strength I needed.

Our friend Janet can be relied upon for unflagging interest and support in all matters Kodiak, but platelets weren't her specialty, either. Kodiak's situation did provide me a good segway to asking about hers; Janet had been recently diagnosed with Multiple Sclerosis, also unfamiliar ground to all of us. It was hard for all of us to hear, hard to believe, hard to accept, but it did explain a lot of things, the weak right hand when she couldn't open the aspirin bottle over the holidays, the double vision. Inflammation is the MS calling card. While the process of discovery and acceptance had been depressing, to say the least, she was approaching it all head on with good humor.

A new symptom, she told me, had surfaced with all kinds of bad timing right while she was conducting a workshop. MS has neck and spine lesions sometimes that send a zing when you lean forward. She'd read about it, we all read those lists of symptoms while we wait for the doctor's pronouncements, but her first experience with it was halfway through a key public presentation. Consequently, the entire workshop could have gone better. I'm sure it was great anyway, but she was feeling pretty low driving home when an odd sensation started on her right side. Again, like a kind of shutter. Or deeper. She started to cry, one more symptom, one more thing to handle. It took a third phone call for her to realize that her cell phone was on vibrate and in her sweater pocket.

Janet laughed. We both laughed. Negative expectations don't help. I'd wait and see what actually was fact with Kodiak and what was just my heavy heart getting in the way.

Friday, March 26

My plane needs sharpening, but it can wait. Kodiak is his old self again, pouncing on invisible mice, inspecting the rock wall for chipmunks, ready for a walk the second I even whisper the word. If I've stayed home from work, why aren't we off tromping our world, he seems to wonder, but then occupies himself in the outdoor world close at hand.

No walk today. The vet had examined all the x-rays, all the tests: spleen, liver, heart, kidneys, all fine. Reflexes, eyes, mental agility, all unchanged. Oxygen count dangerously low. Only a transfusion would tell the tale, so Dr. Balboni brought in his own black lab yesterday. I could have hugged him.

"Any new interest in ducks?" I asked Kodiak, scratching his ears.

If the treatment doesn't kick start his red cell production, the vet had a couple more ideas, but another transfusion wasn't one of them. Too likely to reject it. We'd abandoned the no-human-food rule and had taken to driving Kodes through McDonald's, both a ride and food he was obviously pleased to be offered. Anything to help. I watched him lying like a sphinx, cocking his head to one side at the two-note spring song of the chickadee in his tree. When a hairy woodpecker joined it, he trotted over to the remnant six-inch snow bank under the poplar and checked them out.

 I loved watching him. It was good to be out in shirtsleeves, good to have switched from felt packs to rubber boots. I sat on top of the picnic table, formerly Kodes' favorite perch but lately insurmountable for him, too high, too tiring. Then, he climbed up to join me, a joyous moment. We watched the world together from there. No expectations, no what ifs.

 If the transfusion does nothing else, it will bring Kodiak, David, and me together this coming weekend. No sense wasting precious time with grief. Embrace them while you have them. I snuggled closer. Kodiak lifted his head, and I swear he rolled his eyes a bit and sighed. Okay, I grinned, I'll let you nap. Kodiak has always had a limit to cuddling. He is definitely himself today. Makes it hard to have a heavy heart. Thanks for that, I whispered but pulled back to quit bugging him. He looked up, one ear flipped back, then bounded off. Hard to remember, at this moment, that anything is wrong. Thank you.

Changing Planes

Sunday, April 4th

Minneapolis is shrinking away below me, my first trip without David. Scheduled for months, we had both decided I should still go. I dug deeply to mine a smile. Life goes on, but not always. Only those closest to me at the Great Waters Expo knew what had happened, Minnesota, Montana, and Michigan friends healing a heart broken in Maine.

"I didn't think you'd still come," Tom Helgeson said, "but I think it's good that you did."

Jerry Kustich understood, too, adding, "It doesn't seem like it now, but the space by your knees will be too empty, and you'll need to fill it again."

Ron Barch told me that he'd sent David a well-timed flask in the mail, making us both laugh.

Someone else asked me how my rod was coming along and how was Kodiak?

"My plane needs sharpening," I said.

The cool window against my forehead is as soothing as my view of the endless cloudscape beyond the pane. With empty seats beside me, I can curl up and accept its peace. The mercifully intense last three days have given way to the resigned exhaustion of the long days and nights just before them, our last with Kodes.

Kathy Scott

Such an athlete, such spirit he had.

As the effects of the transfusion wore off, he still insisted on riding to work with David in the back of the truck, his favorite place in the world. The vet marveled at his endurance at noon, saying there might yet be hope for such a strong, fit dog. That evening, Kodiak had been reluctant to come in, lying on the grass watching for squirrels until I finally realized he didn't have the strength to make it those few steps to the house. A strange calm descends with resignation, necessary to face the inevitable. Somehow, we both found the presence to be there for Kodiak, holding his head, watching for signs of any pain that might need our attention. Sometimes there is just no other place you'd rather be in the entire world than sitting on a dog bed with a friend throughout the night.

Before dawn, Kodiak slipped away. We cried, holding him, then carrying him on his dog bed to his truck. With admirable strength and as a perfect tribute to Kodiak's sense of humor and

Changing Planes

joy in life, David drove him through McDonald's one last time on the way to the tears at the Animal Hospital. The vet says that his ashes will be back with us soon. I stayed home to call the people who loved him and let them know.

What better than to drift away in the arms of those who love you?

I believe that, but I sit here crying. Grief catches up in the most awkward places sometimes. Thank goodness for these empty seats. On the clouds, I superimpose the safest of those images, the three of us, home, on his bed together, David cradling Kodiak's weary head, and my face buried in his deep, sweet coat.

Saturday, May 1st

Lost some time, lost in time. Trying to regroup; it is, after all, May Day. Everything is starting over.

I carried my plane blade home from the shop tucked in a vest pocket while I negotiated the path through the pines and warm evening alone in the dark. David arrived closer to nine, having aligned the cork for Hutch's grip to his satisfaction. He placed the heavy Tormac powered-water stone on the floor. It ran at 90 revolutions per minute, purring through the water bath while David explained how to set the gauge to guide for 45-degrees. I was content to watch while he slowly ground the bevel on my blade, a bit wider than the original but it'll be easier for me to sharpen by hand.

Kathy Scott

Monday, May 3rd

Sunday's early sun was hazier than Saturday's with temperatures just a little cooler, but still rose to 77 degrees at midday. The south wind continued a nice breeze which suspended the season one more day before the black fly onslaught.

David and I juggled the things we wanted to do. He had drying splits to put in the twenty new culms of cane, stored for now in the loft of his sister's barn. We decided to drive there to see if he would need help; if not, he'd drive me the mile back to the north house and help me set up to plane my tip strips. The culms proved to be quite manageable, still lying within easy reach on the upper floor and easy to unbundle. I arranged them as they grew, butts together. We marveled at their size and quality. David offered to drive me back until he needed help stashing the cane in the rafters with the fifty other drying culms.

At the north house, I unloaded my writing table, not much of a job, and we carried it out through the sliding doors to the deck just a few feet from its usual place looking out through the glass. We followed with the planing bench platform, decked with a planing form, plane, and a variety of hand tools, orienting everything so I could work my strips and watch the ponds at the same time. David left when he was content that I was all set.

Changing Planes

Felt marker in hand, I hashed the first tip strip with little blue marks roughly three inches apart all down its length, then clamped it in the form using both hands and a leg to open the clamp. David had abandoned these clamps for a simpler system, but their security appealed to me.

I picked up and admired my plane. We had adjusted the bevel on the iron and removed the burred edge, slight but still needing to go. David tested it for the depth of its bite before he left; I tried to memorize the look of the thing, the depth it planed matched to the gap I was seeing. The mouth, adjustable mouth block plane.

Taking a breath, I pulled on my leather gloves. All I had to do was evenly plane off the little blue marks, say, two-thirds of the way down the strip, switch the clamp to the other end, and plane off the remainder. Then I'd redraw the single blue line near the butt of the strip designating, once again, strip one of the tip, then rotate the strip to the other non-enamel facet, and repeat the process, and then back again to the original side.

In between, I needed to suspend the strip between my left forefinger and thumb, measuring it with a digital caliper down its length, spot checking, first one apex to the opposite flat, then the other, making sure the sides still matched. A plane tipped sideways shortens one side and lengthens the other.

Time to dive back in.

I used both hands, one on the bronze cap, cap much too simple a term for such a substantial part, I thought, and one covering the entire front of the plane. The resulting pressure and strength moved the blade through a thin surface layer of bamboo, and a sweet little curl of cane peeled off. A few more passes proved there is such a thing as kinesthetic memory, and I planed pretty much evenly, little blue lines disappearing uniformly, calipers vouching for my efforts.

It was just enough freedom to pay attention to the ponds, too.

From the vantage point high on the deck, looking west, the pond has looked like a small lake ringed with green ever since the level receded. The view is directly downhill under towering white pines to the remnants of the Big Dam, the hundred-foot barrier which yielded to a wind-driven ice floe assault in early spring. That powerful ram split the middle of the dam apart and pushed the two long ends open, great swinging doors we now call jetties, reminiscent of our childhood memories of the Lake Michigan jetties. The breech was so wide that the beavers never considered repairs, concentrating their efforts on reinforcing the North Dam against the torrent of water which roared for days underscoring our lives until the levels of the Big Pond and the North Pond evened out into one odd hourglass-shaped impoundment. Its grasses and sedges are ringed in turn by spruce, and balsam fir, white pine, some tamarack, swamp maples, a few gray beech, and fewer white birch. I'll always be amazed that the North Dam held, but I credit the beavers as well as the bend in the North Pond which prevented the wind-driven ice floe from turning and mounting a direct attack.

By the second strip, I had shed all the clothes I could and still remain modest. While we rarely have visitors, there would be no dog-alert now if someone did approach. No black flies, either, thankfully, and a nice temperature. The sun felt good. Glancing up from my work, I thought that was the general consensus of all present: the buds were bursting out on the maples, red and yellow, and the leaves on the birches were visibly green and longer than squirrels' ears already.

A red squirrel had raided the bird feeder earlier. I had been immersed in a book of Louis Jenkins's poetry when I noticed a movement out the window. The fur all along her back was a rich red in the sunlight. She'd been challenged for the cache of seeds by ten brilliant blue jays, chin-strapped bombers. As she made her escape down the cast iron support pole, I could see she was a nursing mother. The jays were rowdy adolescents, I assumed, teamed up until they found territories or mates. I tapped the window at them to regain her edge and grinned at my lack of compliance with the Non-Intervention Clause, apologies to Star Fleet. She's a bit more used to us than these migrants. Of course, she does keep some of the chickadees, nuthatches, goldfinches, and white-throated sparrows back from the feeder. Pecking order.

Below my planing station, the life of the pond was harder to see in the afternoon's breeze-fed ripples than on quiet mirror mornings and evenings. A pair of mallards dabbled near the shore, just visible below the tall stump left when the crown fell off the old fir last week. High above them, almost twenty-five feet in the air, was an oblong hole in the tree three or four inches long. On the very top of the stump, a drake wood duck in full colors.

Kathy Scott

Across the pond, I knew there were moose tracks amidst the grasses; I'd watched the moose a few hours earlier. It disappeared easily into the North Woods. I had only caught a glimpse, but I thought it was a cow. From the deck, I couldn't see the tracks, but I liked knowing they were there.

David returned just before I planed the last strip, and we decided that I could do them all again before readjusting the planing form. I was coaxing tip strips toward roughly twenty thousandths over the desired butt dimensions, using the same planing form settings I had used to reduce the butt strips. Once the tips matched the butts in size, they'd have a nice initial taper. Then, I'd reset the form, finish the butt strips and reduce the tips again, then reset the form and finish the tips. In theory.

While I marked the first tip strip with little blue lines again and resumed planing, David switched the studded snow tires on the car for the summer tires stored in the woodshed. I could just see the pine-shaded grass where he was working.

I watched for beavers between passes on the strips, but none appeared. Too early in the day, although they've been out in daylight other springs. Beavers live twenty-five years in the wild, barring mishaps, twice that in captivity. The two largest here could have owned this place before we came to steward it. These very beavers may have known us, and Kodiak, for years. The young typically stay with their parents through the next set of siblings, then set off for their own territory when they are two. Four to six kits a year would make for a potential of ten to fourteen beavers in our ponds, except that we seem to have more than one colony now.

Changing Planes

Originally, there were two lodges in the main part of the Big Pond, one more often used. The other, we supposed, was where the female drove the male and older siblings for a few days when she first gave birth to new kits. The little puffballs are so buoyant at birth that they can't submerge even if they slip into the water opening in the floor of the lodge, but they might still be at risk with the others around. Eventually, we knew, the entire family reunites and joins together in the repair and construction of dams, caching of winter food, and the defense of their territory, mostly marking boundaries and tail-slapping at intruders.

After the Big Dam blew open, a lodge which was mostly in disrepair was resurrected in the North Pond, now the north lobe of the hourglass shaped, united bigger pond, and the beavers moved in. The largest we've seen lives there, almost in sight of the deck.

Farther to the south, a half mile upstream through the length of the ponds, is a dam which used to be fragmented. It was grass-covered, hence the Grass Dam. Resurrected, too, to epic proportions, it is now a six-foot tall, eighty-foot long superstructure of gnawed sticks holding a growing South Pond.

A new and very large lodge has appeared in the South Pond. Those beavers, often three, grew accustomed to us before we grew accustomed to finding them there, probable adolescents who had known us downstream for two and a half years. By contrast, the smaller beavers with the large one to the north are still pretty wary - last year's kits. We still haven't seen new kits in either pond.

Kathy Scott

The great expanse of the original Big Pond in between the lodges still has active beavers, although I still can't tell if they are residing in the two lodges there, somewhat high and dry, or visiting from the north and south. If they are residents, the total number of beavers would increase in my tally by anywhere from two to eight. That would also put their kits in very close proximity to the otter we saw last week and the mink we've seen in the past, both potential predators. There are a few snapping turtles, too. Beavers have more problems than I'd originally thought. I wonder if they are bothered by the red-spotted green leeches, the graceful ribbons of the ponds, or if their fur is too thick, their feet and tail too much like leather.

Every lodge has remnants of a winter food cache, but that's still not proof of residence. Beavers are industrious but pretty habitual and a little sloppy. They work in response to programming, cache here, repair there. If their guard hairs detect water movement, patch the hole with mud, grass, sticks. If a tree under tooth starts to crack inside, run! Their hearing is amazing, their eyesight keyed to movement, but I suspect there is no real planning, no real plan, even. In the summer, when the guard hairs are shed, the urge to dam diminishes as does the chance of damage to dams caused by spring melt water. It all works out.

I stopped to measure my last strip, setting aside thoughts of beavers for awhile. Time flies. Even suspended time flies. Already, David had the tires changed, the snows stored. We drove back to his sister's barn to select three culms to bring home for the next rods, the Rapid River donation rod first. We're joining with our Internet friends from the Flyfishinginmaine.com bulletin board in attempting to rescue the wild brook trout in the Rapid from the onslaught of invasive species.

After storing the rest of the cane in the loft, we were both a little hungry. I checked the paper to find that *Touching the Void* was playing in Farmington. How about a good Peruvian mountaineering documentary and movie theater popcorn? We stashed my table and tools inside, washed up, and made the four o'clock matinee. It's still strange to go off at will and on a whim. When we drive the truck, his favorite, we still think of Kodiak as being in the back, with us.

Afterwards, we had time to pull on rubber boots and make our way around the pond in the twilight. The wind was picking up. We found one beaver swimming across the northern lobe and flushed six wood ducks, the pair of mallards, and a lone black duck. We didn't see the moose, but we knew where she was. She'd been eating the new buds on the young maples just north of the house when we drove by on our way to the show.

Kathy Scott

Thursday, May 13th

After our daily walk around the ponds, where the black flies are still conspicuously absent, the painted trilliums are in bloom, the deer and moose tracks abound, and the geese are quite vocal, I planed the tip strips closer to the surface of the planing form, twenty thousandths of an inch over the butt dimensions. As cane shaves away, I'm worried about planing off the steel of the form here and there, as well as the growing possibility of a planing accident. What if I peel up an edge and tear a bamboo strip down beyond my taper?

David paused from roughing the finish between Sean's fourth and fifth coats of spar urethane to help me readjust the blade so I wouldn't hog off so much cane that I'd get a tear-out, as well as save the poor planing form from the wounds I might inflict. Even with the slotted plane base I'd nicked the form a bit and stopped to sand it smooth.

I tried it again, marking all of the strips and then planing down their lengths. How even with the planing form's surface is even? I ran my fingers from steel across cane across the steel, from one side across my strip to the other side, trying to determine if they made a single level surface. Maybe not, but maybe tonight's not the night to try again. I want my strips as close to perfect as possible; pushing on when I'm tired or, admittedly, somewhat chicken, won't help. I bundled the strips in order, wound string in a spiral down the bundle and back up, and brushed the shavings off the table into a paper bag for stove tinder. After these tips, the next step will be to coax the butt strips even with the planing form surface, then set the form for the final butt dimensions.

Saturday, May 15th

The truth was right there in front of me. The bound tip strips, when laid side-by-side with the butt strips, were visibly bigger. That's not how it's supposed to work. I had been ready to switch back to planing the butts, but David advised me to change my plans, keep those strips on hold for now and continue to plane the tips. He thought I might be a bit too cautious. He assured me that their final dimension is smaller than the butts, so with the form still set for the butt dimensions I shouldn't be able to shave off too much. He said not to worry about the planing form (it is steel, it is mine, I don't care), and that it would be good to keep practicing before making final, irreversible passes on the butts.

All good points.

Starting again with tip strip number one, I planed more off both non-enamel sides. They were beginning to look like something, a rod tip maybe, and curiosity took hold. Instead of rebinding them with string, I taped the tip strips into a hexagon, a foreshadow of their look as a blank, a decision I regretted the moment I picked up the butt strips. Instead of using string, these had been taped while waiting, probably less of an issue if they hadn't been left in the dry heat so long. When I peeled off the tape which had been holding them, a gooey smudge remained.

Kathy Scott

No way I wanted to put that into the precise V of the planing form. I called for assistance, and David showed me how to dissolve away the goo with acetone and wipe off the residue. I made a mental note to get back to the tips as soon as possible, preferably before their tape could deteriorate.

I dug out the paperwork and examined the final settings for the butt strips, numbers, it turned out, that I couldn't match on the planing form. The form, being designed to achieve a variety of tapers for a variety of rod lengths, extended much longer than necessary for this tiny fly rod. I'd chosen a section of it to use and marked stations accordingly. Now, I slid the depth indicator along the groove, loosening and tightening bolts and pushpins until I was convinced that my spring allergies weren't affecting my perception. The form just wouldn't respond. I hated to ask David.

I asked David. He checked the form, and it was in fact at the smallest settings that section of the form could take. He showed me how to adjust where I'd written all of the numbers on the masking tape adjacent to the form, the half diameter settings, effectively moving the workstation toward the end of the planing form with the smaller V. Such a simple fix. I decided to blame my allergies after all.

Adjusting the form again, this time to the new stations, I immediately ran into the same roadblock. The form closed tight, and still the V wasn't small enough. Calmer and wiser now, I looked it over. I had five extra inches of planing form left, so I transcribed the settings one more station toward the very end of the form, crossed my fingers, and started adjusting it again. David had said to avoid flipping the form over to its finer side if

Changing Planes

I could, and, while I wasn't sure of his reasoning, I had none of my own to substitute. Fortunately, the planing form responded nicely, and I was able to set the final dimensions for my butt strips along the section running to the very end.

By then, the hour was late and my allergies were reaching that intolerable nuisance state, so we both decided that I was in no shape for precision work. Planing the butt strips would have to wait until tomorrow, maybe until the pollen receded or the first cleansing rain. Maybe a couple days. Maybe longer. We've reluctantly accepted that we have all the freedom in the world, now. With summer coming, who knew what that would mean?

Kathy Scott

On a river without a fly rod, I'm a tourist.
Rod in hand, I become something more.

~ David James Duncan

Changing Planes

Friday, August 6th

We stopped for caribou burgers at the Whaler Restaurant on the southern coast of Labrador. We'd already eaten pan-fried cod which had been swimming the day before for less money than the cost of a fast food meal at home. Grilled cheese sandwiches were priced higher than moose burgers, both around four dollars Canadian; the caribou was just a dollar more. Amazing meals at amazing prices in an amazing land.

Labrador.

We were back in Red Bay, once an old Basque whaling village, visited twice now in as many days. While we dined, sea fog dramatically masked and then reveled a derelict ship rusting in the harbor, then the narrow passage that is the Strait of Belle Isle, and then, more distant, the northern shore of Newfoundland. The tundra and tuckamore surrounded the town as if it was sitting on a mountaintop. Out the window from our small table, a wooden boardwalk marked the trail to a windswept granite summit. Beneath and beside its steps lay whitened whalebones and clumps of orange bakeapples. Bakeapple tarts, bakeapple pies, bakeapple jellies; they've been in every shop, a jewel harvested near the lingering snow patches in August. Red Bay marks the northern terminus of the paved road, a road we'd just followed on as gravel all the way to its end at the ferry dock in Cartwright. We were still wide-eyed on this return stop, making our way back to our ferry, soon back to the island half of the province.

The news was just as intriguing as the landscape as we drove back along the Strait, where just this week two couples had been boating, according to the CBC. They'd cut the motor to photograph the cliffs, drifting acoustically invisible to the passing whales. One breached, came down on the boat's windshield and the boater's wife, the latter now finally conscious in the hospital. The boater, the radio said, was understandably concerned. The last time he'd vacationed with his wife, she'd been struck by lightning. We decided to gracefully refuse any invitation to join them, should our paths ever cross.

Paths do cross in these places.

After we'd purchased our fishing license two weeks earlier, just off the ferry from Nova Scotia to the southeast corner of Newfoundland, we'd found a campsite and read over the regulations. We were, we told ourselves, on a reconnaissance run, discovering the lay of the Maritimes for a next visit with more fishing. Too late in the summer, we suspected, for great fishing this trip and, even for the committed explorers that we sometimes are, too much territory to scout. Still, exploration being only half the fun, a little fishing could fit in. We fronted, in amazement, the thirteen dollars Canadian for a family seasonal license for trouting, but the information clerk at Marine Atlantic seemed even more surprised that we'd actually want to fish for trout and had no advice for us. We awakened to the sound of the ocean through the windswept firs, showered at what turned out to be a characteristically wonderful Newfoundland Provincial Park free shower, and were enjoying breakfast amidst the bunchberries and pitcher plants when that same Marine Atlantic clerk tracked us down, miles away. He'd found out about the trouting, if we were still interested.

After two weeks of similar encounters, we weren't a bit surprised when we returned to Labrador's Pinware Provincial Park and the ranger waved us on to camp as regulars; we'd just camped there two nights before. As with out first stay, the well-sheltered campsites were all deserted except for impossible hordes of blackflies, while the campers swarmed the picnic area parking lot on the spit of land caressed by the saltwater breeze. We recognized two of the rigs, Annie and Bill from Connecticut and Anne and Bruce from Vermont. Old friends, they were traveling together and waved us over to their picnic table under a screen tent as companions reunited. Like hikers do on the Appalachian Trail or RVs in the long caravan that follows the Alaska Highway, we'd crossed their path more than once already.

We were still in Newfoundland and looking for brook trout the first time we saw them. Trout, though, were proving elusive. We knew we'd need to hire a guide to fish for Atlantic salmon anywhere, but we hadn't expected them to be everywhere. We took a side road toward Burgeo, pausing in wonder at each breath-taking river, majestic and a fitting home for such a stately creature as these salmon, long troubled in Maine, endangered, we knew. We'd often fished their landlocked cousins, and there was rumor of one or two caught and either released or poached in the Kennebec River each year, but we'd never seen an Atlantic in the wild until we stood on the cliff above the Humber River. The unreasonable grandeur stirred a deep, unyielding empathy as we imagined the Atlantics diving to the very depths of the great pool at the base of the falls and then leaping up the torrent. We held our breath and watched for them in the long engineered V-shaped trench that Lee Wulff worried would rob the river of selecting for passage only the strongest, only the most fit. We'd have settled for seeing a parr. A great splashing in the shallow rapids above the falls caught our eyes, and there it was, a fierce salmon battling the current long enough for photos that would later put truth to our claims that it was over three feet long and beautiful. Surely it was a sight like this that made Wulff realize that these Atlantic salmon are too precious to be caught only once.

Finally, somewhere along a small but beautifully graveled stream, we pulled in. There was no sign proclaiming it a scheduled salmon river, a river restricted to fishing with guides and a salmon license. We tucked the truck into a grove of spruce, geared up, and waded in. One, two, we each caught an Atlantic salmon. Thrilled then guilt-stricken, we released them, and then continued catching their siblings, all parr, all between six and ten inches long. We tried the pool, or steady, and then the narrow, faster water at its foot, the tickle, until we released a similar sized, sparkling brook trout. We retreated to the truck to find we had company at the impromptu campsite, but before we could mourn our loss of solitude, they offered us fresh raspberry pie with cream and tales of local wildlife politics that we couldn't resist. The next morning, we resolved to explore to the north of the island until we found a perfect and unscheduled trout stream.

We drove all the way to the top of Newfoundland.

Along the way, we made notes of things important: dramatic scheduled salmon rivers, thick and hot mooseburgers (moose on the side of the road, moose in ponds, moose in the road), tiny garden plots of potatoes planted in the fertile fill along the highway, never-ending incredible scenery (deep fjords, moonscape hidden valleys, rocky mountainsides, dense spruce bogs), whalebacks (both mammalian and granite), tiny colorful villages, a McDonald's (two sundaes for two dollars), and an amazing variety of potato chips. We tried chips with ketchup, chips with vinegar, and chips with gravy.

 The road led to L'Anse aux Meadows, a settlement steeped in history. The little fishing village was still quite isolated until the 1960s, even the coastal ferry system bypassed it. The park interpreter told us that he and everyone had been surprised when a boat came ashore with two Norwegians asking about ruins. The villagers all recognized the features the visitors described. The interpreter himself played on the long low rises without a thought as to what they were. After a few years of careful but brief summer excavations, proof was found of Norse inhabitation: some smelted nails, some rivets, a man's shoulder-cloak pin. Curious, we made our way into one of the reconstructed sod-covered longhouses to hear the tale.

 A costumed local assuming the role of a Viking settler was engaged in a lively discussion with a stautesque tourist whose long ponytail was adorned with feathers. Both were knowledgeable and seemed to thrive on the matching of wits and historical interpretation, much to our benefit. Their insights volleyed back and forth. Bog iron from Black Duck Creek (which our Montana rodmaking friend Jerry Kustich had told us contained trout) wasn't of sufficient quality to produce a great number of nails easily. A sewing needle and yarn whorl pointed to the presence of women. The only child of the seventy-five inhabitants, the first white child of Europeans born in North America, Snorri, may have been Leif Ericson's son, they thought. The two men debated whether this could well have been the mysterious Norse Vinland, but while one pointed to the evidence of the twenty miles of beach indicated on ancient map and currently present in nearby Labrador as proof, the other felt that since there were no grapes present and the distances involved were nothing to Norsemen (Greenland to Baffin Island and then south being far shorter than the 1,400 miles from Norway had been), this site was just a jumping off point to Vinland, and that's why the settlement was abandoned.

They drove it home to us; we needed to head north.

We booked passage across the Strait of Belle Isle and lined up the next morning in the drizzle to wait to board the ferry at St. Barbe. We found our place, by chance, right at the edge of the wharf, keeping warm and dry in the truck without sacrificing the view. The rain poured down by the time the ship approached the dock and used its side thrusters to sidle in. The strong jets of water worked magic; an Atlantic salmon answered an innate call to leap and shot out of the ocean next to the ferry. We both saw it. If there is a good omen for a Labrador ferry crossing, that had to be it.

We were a bit dismayed to find the campground on the Pinware virtually closed due to black flies, but the silver lining was a hearty welcome into a screen tent near the beach. We ducked into to the bug free-haven to find the feathered historian and his wife and friends eager to share both bug-spray and a veritable feast. They were of indomitable spirit and traveled with a long-haired German shepherd and a chattering parakeet. The truck and fifth-wheel trailer belonged to Bill and Annie; Bill had grown up in Maine, attended college near us, and drew beautifully, but Annie was the artist. Their friends were from Vermont, retired, and occupying the modest pick-up camper parked nearby. They told us they were sight-seeing but made it seem like a spiritual pilgrimage; we told them that we were scouting for brook trout streams perfect for cane rods.

"Really," Bill pondered, not actually asking a question. "Tell me more about cane rods."

We left for Cartwright early in the morning, stopping in Red Bay for our first time around noon. From there, the gravel road which led north was so wide and smooth that we could drive our four wheel drive pick-up truck at speeds approaching fifty miles per hour and I could still use an ink pen. The tundra, with its snow patches, pink granite, and bakeapples, gave way to endless spruce and fir. We passed modest lakes not on our maps and remarkable lakes with floatplanes and calling loons. Mary's Harbor sheltered a Grenfell Mission and school (Home of the Wolves), as well as the ferry we'll take some day to Battle Harbor. Despite an almost an overwhelming amount to see, we kept focused until we found the potential perfect stream.

Around 4:30, we pulled to one side of the wide gravel road. We'd yet to see a vehicle. I pulled on my bug jacket in the truck, tucked it in at the waist, cinched up the wrists, and tucked my pantlegs into my socks, taking care to wear a billed hat underneath to hold the net away from my face and not to dress too warmly. David took a similar but more sane approach. Then we chose my rod, the first David ever made, looped on one of my leaders and some tippet, and tied on an olive bodied tan caddis. We decided whose turn it was to try the water first (his) and slid down the steep roadside to the stream.

The pool was deep, flowing over gravel and emptying as a lively stream shaded by alders. One cast, fly snatched, brook trout caught, admired, released. Easy as that. Stunning. My turn, the same result. We alternated the rod for one hour, twelve trout, three of size with kyped jaws. I caught the alders a few times trying to cast underneath, but they were as generous as the trout were willing. I only lost one fly. Brook trout, on cane, in Labrador. Some silvery, most vivid and beautiful. They were all wild, all feisty.

We explored northward, looking not just for streams but for a way to pull off the gravel for the night. The construction crews left considerable ditches to consume the great amounts of snow they likely plow. The elevated road had a drawback for opportunistic campers, though, and it was late before we found a roadwork staging area where we could sleep.

The black flies didn't seem to realize that the breeze racing between the stored culverts and fuel drums was supposed to drive them away, not into our truck. I escaped from those outside to find more inside, killing one hundred and eleven before the dark descended and some relatively polite mosquitoes flew in as tag-team replacements. David smoked a cigar before retreating far into his sleeping bag, but I reasoned that I had no blood left anyway and kept my nose out in the cool northern air, one hand free, sacrificed for swatting. Neither of us slept much, but it made for an early start the next day.

Changing Planes

We followed the rolling terrain of the Paradise River through dark conifers until we came to the little hunting and fishing camps of the village, each with its own pickup truck and wood pile. Before seven, we had our first view of Cartwright, small white houses sloping down a low hill to a breathtaking Arctic bay. Beautiful. There were dories along shore, beached by the tide. Picturesque crab trap piles. A big John Deere double snow blower, an Eagle River Trail Association groomer. A clinic. Roasted chicken flavored potato chips. A hair salon in a house (there's one in every village, I think). The ferry from Cartwright to Happy Valley/Goose Bay is always booked months ahead, although that may change when the new parallel road carries traffic between them. With four hundred fifteen kilometers between us and our ferry, we turned around.

"Welcome back," Bill greeted us when we returned to the campsite on the Pinware. He waved us over. They were going to that evening's Bakeapple Festival and hoped we'd come along so we could talk. I've never seen a province so full of festivals, so fond of music as Newfoundland and Labrador, on the ferries, in the kitchens, live and lively in the streets. But we were both road weary, maybe a bit exsanguinated, so we gratefully declined.

"In the morning, then," Bill asked, "could you wait to leave until we've talked?"

We agreed, but, in comparing plans, we had reservations for the same ferry they hope to board on stand-by. One way or another, our paths would continue to be intertwined.

Kathy Scott

With our truck oriented to catch the wind from the strait, we passed the evening immersed in the magic of Labrador. The spit of sand and spruce was actually the dividing line between the freshwater Pinware River and the saltwater of the strait, scheduled fishing for salmon to our left, free fishing (no license, any tackle) on our right. We talked at length with the ranger, local by his accent (lab-bra-DOOR, new-fund-LAND), who said you can't miss on the Pinware salmon run the first week of July, maybe the first three, and that the Lucky Strike Lodge is the best lodge. I liked his loyalty. He swore that they always catch Arctic char right from the wharf just north in Charlotteville this time of year, but not with flies.

In fact, he told us, William Anderson from Nain, a little farther north, had been pulling a char net out yesterday using a seventeen foot canoe with a twenty-horsepower motor when the mooring wrapped around the throttle. He was thrown into the frigid water. Unable to swim the two hundred feet to the wharf, he crawled up on the flipped canoe and called for help. No one heard him. He told himself not to panic and tried to paddle with his hands toward shore. After forty-five minutes, the ranger said, he was pretty tired, but he was rescued. The RCMP, the Royal Canadian Mounted Police, helped him flip the canoe over and get the water out, then towed it to Nain. It could have been worse, Anderson had said. He had fixed the motor, the story continued, then had gone back out today. He had reported that he got a real good haul in his net. In fact, there were so many char, he had brought the net in. There's a lot of char, he had said.

Changing Planes

    The ranger told us other stories, too, all the news. Poachers were caught with one thousand salmon from the pools on the Humber which were closed right now, the water levels too low. The little cabins we'd seen lining the bays were winter houses where locals used to gather for the length of that long season, now vacation homes. Two hikers lost in the Torngats were found dead even though they'd had a satellite phone. The cod moratorium of 1989 helped, but most locals still fish only near shore for small quantities. There were guys with big nets who used to raise them just high enough to snag hundreds of Atlantic salmon as by-catch, a very desirable and profitable "accident".

    We munched on smoke and barbeque flavored potato chips and lingered in our last Labrador night, walking the sand to the end of the spit and back, planning for the morning before the ferry. Every conversation, it seemed, led back to Atlantic salmon in the end.

    There are so many way-of-life changes in Labrador and just across the waves in Newfoundland, glowing in the day's last light. Although we live relatively close to Maritime Canada, we'd never crossed by ferry to Newfoundland because we thought the passage too grueling for Kodiak. Things change. One chapter closes, but the next chapter continues the story. So rare and precious to see sunsets over the Atlantic for people from Maine, where Atlantic sunrises are treasures. It seems we share more with these people than shores of the same ocean. I wonder about the way of life in Maine and what the future holds.

    The interpreter at L'anse aux Meadows grew up there in the tiny village, playing on Norse foundation mounds as a child. He remembers the arrival of the scientists. Now, instead of an isolated fishing community, he's part of the world cultural heritage community, with access via a fine paved road and travelers daily, hourly, from across Canada and around the world, accompanied by all of the businesses which serve them. Small shops, bed and breakfasts, kayak charters to see whales, hiking excursions to see caribou, rumors of incredible salmon fishing: I'd thought at the time that an entire vacation right there couldn't last long enough.

But it is a different path than he'd expected.

Maybe it was easier, David thought, with the decline of the cod fishery. The switch from fishing to tourism softened the collapse of the cod market and the accompanying hardships, we'd been told, although I can't say everyone embraced it as a preference. Survival. I wonder about all of the locals, seemingly impervious to black flies, out on the barrens in shorts and tank tops harvesting bakeapples; were they stocking their own cupboards or converting them to currency through new ventures like the Dark Tickle jams and jellies enterprise? And where do Atlantic salmon and brook trout fit in with this type of survival of the fittest?

Atlantic salmon, it turned out, couldn't survive harvesting any better than the cod and were probably more fragile. Lee Wulff said it early, and by the 1960's, when L'Anse aux Meadows was "discovered," catch and release was gaining some mention. Still, Atlantic salmon being caught off Greenland by Newfoundland and Labrador commercial interests continued through a decreasing local limit and stricter regulation. That the interests of the quantity-oriented fishers opposed those of the outfitters and lodge owners eventually became obvious. How could people wed to the mass-harvesting of ocean fish be expected to embrace catch and release, or, say, the taking of one or two Atlantic salmon on flies per year? The lodges said they could employ a number of people and harvest dollars from the tourists anglers who'd even come for mud trout, as brook trout were often called, and hoped for regulations to bolster that species. A twelve fish daily limit and the price of $13 for a family non-resident season trout license hardly seems like an implicit cry for protection at this point. On the other hand, guides are required for salmon fishing, a protection of guides maybe, but some protection for the fish, too. It's easy to see that both politics and conservation continue to evolve here.

In Maine, too. When new regulations were proposed for the Kennebec, there was quite a stir. People don't let go of their heritage easily or without good reason. Hell hath no fury like a tradition scorned. Maine's Atlantic salmon population was in trouble, we knew, although it had seemed less personal until now. The fish of kings is everyone's fish in Newfoundland. We'd been involved in conservation efforts to restore habitat, to fight the encroachment of development or invasive species in Maine's brook trout waters, most recently the efforts to save the brook trout of the Rapid River. But salmon, we'd have to look into them more. Other than the Edwards Dam coming out on the Kennebec, and a couple rumors of Atlantics caught accidentally, what is going on?

Maybe it's time to go home and find out.

Kathy Scott

Saturday, August 28

No longer the travelers, home and the tables are turned; we observed a couple of surprise visitors today, both travelers just passing through. The first was a white morph great blue heron. Just at sunrise, we found it strolling in the Big Pond over on the west side. It was beautiful right side up and in the mirrored reflection, but certainly unusual. Since we'd seen them in Florida and the remnants of Hurricane Charley were headed our way, we wondered if it might have ridden the tropical winds north. We'd been on the phone almost constantly, first accessing the threat to my Mom and my stepfather Archie in Fort Myers, then locating them once they fled. Safely across the state, they were without ready communication, so we tracked down neighbors for them until we heard of the big pine now reclining across their carport, power lines, and shed. My brother loaded a generator and sped down from North Carolina, fixing them up with air conditioning and a cell phone as the utilities slowly mended. With Hurricane Frances a potential follow-up threat, they're considering a flight north. Maybe this heron had the right idea. A small duck or teal swam behind the heron toward the cattails, distracting its Jurassic attention momentarily.

Later, we stopped by the Oosoola Store in Norridgewock for pizza. We have a long history of ordering the same pizza there, half hamburger, half pepperoni, and then saving the last sliver of pepperoni for Kodiak. He was rarely allowed human food, but a reward for waiting patiently outside seemed the least we could do, and it had become a tradition.

We parked on the side of the building where the shade would spread as we lunched and had just stepped out of the truck when David waved to the road.

"Look at that truck!" he said, hand raised.

I turned to see who'd be waving back, but the sun was in the driver's eyes so he couldn't easily see us. The camper did look vaguely familiar. There was an unmistakable green license plate.

"Wasn't that the truck driven by Bill and Annie's friends, the people from Vermont we met with them in Labrador?" Of course it was. Route 2 is the best way back, whether you love two lane highways, as they had said they did, or not. No freeway goes from Atlantic Canada through Maine to Vermont. Still, what are the odds that we'd be here and looking just as they drove by? One another of Life's inside jokes, and the second surprise in one day.

We retrieved our pizza from John at the counter, caught up briefly on his summer news and ours, then sat by the windows in the dining area and flipped the box open. We each started with a hamburger slice. Fueled with pizza and the odd chance of the Vermont camper passing by, our talk returned to Labrador.

Bill had found us early the morning we were all due to cross the strait back to Newfoundland. Since they didn't have reservations, they were going to caravan with their friends to the ferry and wait there until one of the crossings had openings for their fifth wheel and the Vermont camper. If our paths didn't cross again, he wanted to make sure he asked us a bamboo fly rod question. Annie's uncle had recently passed away leaving her, among other things, a cane rod. They weren't really sure what to do with it. The rod had been a favorite, but Annie didn't fish and Bill hadn't since he had left Maine, so they were out of touch with such things.

We talked at length, there on the Pinware, of the personal and the market values of various fly rods, their condition, lengths, and weights. Bill mulled it over philosophically, saying there was much to consider. They moved off to the ferry's standby waiting line, and we toured the tiny villages in between. We munched on bakeapple tarts while listening to the CBC (11,000 new jobs in Newfoundland this year, bringing unemployment down to 15%). A Labrador wildlife officer from Cartwright had released a new CD, singing "Shantytown, by the shore, I've come home to you once more," an instant hit with us.

At L'Anse-Amour, we followed a small road out to see a lighthouse, which turned out to be the Point Armour lighthouse, the tallest in the province, but we found much more. A little sign told us a small mound of rocks marked the site of the oldest known burial in North America, a Maritime Archaic twelve-year-old child lying face down these last 7,500 years. A tiny local cemetery lay just beyond it near eight tidy little houses; near that, the final resting place of Basque whalers from the 1500's. The dirt road continued between cliff and shore, beautiful, but marked with another sign. We stood over the ocean and read that the beach was considered dangerous, littered still with live World War II ordinance. Amazing, we thought, how often does anyone come here that no one has taken care of sixty year old shells? The lighthouse was a part of a compound of five white buildings with red tops, the tower impressive, striking, with a bold black stripe two thirds of the way to the top and a crowning red roof. We stood below it to read the interpretive sign. Another surprise, it read 530 million year old fossilized reef. Looking to the water below, we recognized the same green rock with distinct white circles we'd seen at the ancient grave. Fossilized sponges from millions of years ago.

We could have gone home right then; we were beginning to lapse into wonderment overload. But the ferry wouldn't leave for hours even to Newfoundland, still far from home, so we drove past the terminal to discover that isolated Quebec villages are every bit as amazing as their Labrador counterparts.

When we finally pulled in line to board the ferry, Bill and Annie's fifth wheel and Bruce and Anne's pickup camper were right there with us. We six reunited in the forward lounge, conversation flowing freely on the crossing. Our plan was to travel more or less directly home, hoping to be in Maine before Hurricane Charley was in Florida just in case the family needed us. Bill and Annie were headed toward Connecticut at a more leisurely but direct pace, and Bruce and Anne were free to dawdle.

"We've been thinking about that cane rod," Bill told us. "Annie and I believe it is a Leonard, bought new, maybe in the fifties. We wondered if you'd like to have it?"

David and I immediately misunderstood. "We really aren't in a position to collect rods," David explained. "That's one of the reasons I make them." We laughed at the standard impoverished-rodmaker joke.

"Actually," Bill told us, "we were thinking the rod should be with someone who'd appreciate it. We'd like to give it to you."

This was too much.

"Bill," David said, "we can't take that rod. You might be able to get some good money for it." He paused. "I could ask around for you."

Bill and Annie weren't dissuaded so easily. "Pay us when and whatever you like, then," Bill said.

"First, let's see what you have," David decided. "We could direct you to someone who would appreciate it and pay you what it's worth. It would be easier if I could see the rod, though." He gave Bill our address and they agreed that Bill would send pictures.

We made our way more or less directly back to one of the Provincial Parks we'd visited earlier, albeit rather late at night. The ranger didn't mind us arriving after hours, but like everyone in Newfoundland, it seemed, recognized us and wondered how the fishing had been. We explained that exploring came first, although we had wanted to christen our cane rods on Newfoundland and Labrador brook trout and we had.

"Cane?" he asked, interested. "Bamboo fly rods? I saw one last year."

We didn't pay for the night until we were checking out the next morning. A new ranger was at the office, but she said, "Oh, you must have the cane rods. Sheldon asked if you could stop by the gatehouse on the way out."

Changing Planes

We did. David and the ranger who had become Sheldon stood outside talking in a small swarm of black flies which would surely recognize that I had just showered my bug dope off. They cast every rod we had in the truck, talked about its taper, decided what would be best for Sheldon's local waters.

As we waved good-bye, David told me that Sheldon was also a guide, like nearly everyone who fishes, Sheldon claimed, and that we should come back and stay at his place the second week of July. He'd guide us for the fun of it, he knew where there were lots of the nice medium sized salmon he preferred to the spawners in his home town, and we'd all use cane. He usually lived in L'Anse aux Meadows.

David and I finished the second slices of pizza, the half with pepperoni. We cleared off the table, tucked the soda bottles into the recycling bin, and stopped to deposit the pizza box. In it, we'd left one small slice of pepperoni. Kodiak's piece. We looked at each other, both suddenly teary-eyed, and laughed.

"We've got to stop missing him so much," I said. "I can't take being bush wacked like this," all the while trying to smile.

David was practical. "Maybe we should just switch to another kind of pizza. Might be easier."

Inside, though, the idea was growing. I knew there was a third choice.

Kathy Scott

To me, to live without dogs
would mean accepting a form
of blindness.

~ Thomas McGuane

Changing Planes

Sunday, August 29th

Ah, the best laid plans.

Finally a moment and the inclination, and it's too hot and muggy to plane. We decided to organize the shop a bit instead, first arranging David's work spaces for binding, gluing, lathe work, wrapping, and planing, then by sorting, labeling, and storing in drawers all of his guides, reel seats, and ferrules, then the reels and silk lines, then the sandpapers sorted by grit, and then things we found when those places were clear.

We substituted two small wooden children's school desks, discards, as legs replacing my sawhorses and a beautiful birch library table top, also a discard, for my old workbench. My furling board fits with plenty of room in front of my elevated planing platform, now nested at the back of the tabletop. I can easily switch them to resume planing. I'd like to start soon.

Recreation, especially travel, is well named. Re-creation. If the fact that we're organizing the shop isn't evidence enough, our rekindled spirits are bursting out all over. The most telltale sign of all: I didn't run and hide at this week's meeting of the directors of our Trout Unlimited chapter, the one where they start discussing officers.

These are hard working, solid, conservation-minded anglers. I am in constant awe of the things they do, the things they know. That the Kennebec River is free-flowing all the way in from the Atlantic at Merrymeeting Bay to the Lockwood

Dam at Waterville is a direct result of some of the people who sit once a month around the tables upstairs in Mike Holt and Linda Clark's fly shop, the Directors, selflessly volunteering their time for restoration and education projects, helping with my middle school students, surveying streams, lobbying the State for increased fish passage. They do it with good humor and with good sense.

    I so value their knowledge and insights that we lingered after the meeting talking Atlantic salmon restoration over a tailgate in the parking lot. Greg Ponte would be inviting someone from Maine's Atlantic Salmon Commission to speak to us soon. With cutbacks in funding, we could buoy the State's restoration efforts with a bit of hard work. There was the dam on the Sandy River to consider, too, the dam near us in Mercer. If it came out, that entire river would be free flowing from its headwaters in the mountains to the Kennebec.

    These guys knew things, as always, and I was playing catch up. David had paid dues to the Atlantic Salmon Federation for some time, but time itself had been an obstacle in getting more involved. The Chapter, we were assured, needed an ASF representative, we were an affiliated club. Appointing one would be one of the tasks of a new president, now that we had term limits (the sitting president, Sean, thought of that). Then they all looked at me.

Changing Planes

Saturday, September 25

On Monday, I saw the puppies on the Internet. I typed in three words, free puppies Maine, then followed some links and landed at PAWS, a rescue shelter in Calais. Rhoda and Ruby had been found by a truant officer searching an abandoned trailer, frightened puppies in a cardboard box, when the shelter took them in. Two weeks later, they were favorites, the shelter's description said, both the sweetest and the most well-behaved pups they'd seen. Their pictures were adorable-black muzzles, silky ears, bright dark eyes. German shepherd - husky crosses, they were guessing. Both had black coats and black feathery tails, but Ruby's forehead, ears, and legs were tan and her feet and the tip of her tail were white. A white spot fell just off center on her black nose. Rhoda was mostly black with cream eyebrows and cheeks and long cream legs. In the picture, she looked like a skinny waif, but a spunky one.

They were both melt-your-heart cute.

I couldn't even send the link to David - it would be too hard to say no to them so quickly. I mentioned the pups that night, testing the water, and sent the link the next day. On Wednesday, I filled out an application detailing all the things careful shelters want to know: what jobs we had, if the yard was fenced (no, I finally wrote, reluctantly, then added that we have one hundred acres to offer them, ample space off an infrequently traveled dirt road), how we planned to train them, when we'd walk them, our list of references. References? Would they really read all this? Would they really call? But without the paperwork, we couldn't ask more questions about the pups, the shelter understaffed for the mountain of work it had to do. We needed to get on The List first. That made me laugh; rodmakers these days know about waiting lists. Still, our chances didn't seem sure, so I searched the Internet a little more. There was a five month old pup in Farmingdale, too. That shelter wanted a home visit.

David said that taking both pups was a thought. I sent in a lengthy packet.

On Friday, PAWS actually called our vet, as well as Janet in Michigan and our other references from work (no input from relatives allowed), and then called me at noon. When I called David, buried at work, he was lukewarm, and our evening spent digging through Kodiak's things disintegrated into tears. We thought of all of the questions we should ask about the puppies and those we should ask of ourselves. Would two be twice as hard as one? Would rescuing two at once afford us some solace if we left them behind but together on a major trip? What if their early life had scarred their health? What if…

It was as exhausting as it was sad. Our lives had only just changed; were we ready to change again? In the wee hours of the morning, I almost decided to call PAWS to tell them that it was just too soon.

Almost.

By 6 a.m., we were on the road to Calais just to look at the pups. Calais (pronounced in Maine like callous, not like its French namesake) is right on the Maritime border with Canada, a New Brunswick border town with a little of the North Woods frontier flavor about three hours from us. The shelter there did its best, but had no separate quarters for puppies. Ruby and Rhoda were running more or less loose with one hundred and ten unlikely roommates. Leggy and adorable, they tore through the cat room and claimed us. We really didn't stand a chance.

It has been a week today.

Over seven days, there have been the beginnings of the lessons of life with us, things they need to learn, things we need to learn: where it's okay to "Go potty", sleeping happens between 10 p.m. and 5 a.m. (in the puppy proof kitchen of the north house) but that we'll switch from the south house to sleeping nearby just in case a puppy needs to go out at 2:30 a.m.. We're slowly moving away from their interim life as cats, too, although it's handy to be able to call "here, kitty-kitty-kitty" and have them come running.

Kathy Scott

The stars have been overwhelmingly bright this week, one falling last night and illuminating a trail we four looked up to see.

We've tried a couple of test rides in their metal crate in the back of the truck with marginal results. Midge, the inquisitive pup formerly known as Rhoda who bugged us constantly on that first ride home in the car and is named for both the pesky insect and our affection for Paul Young cane rods, seems fine in the truck, but our brown tone Effie, named for rodmaker F. E. Thomas, is so nervous in the truck that she wet their bed in the crate.

Having two together seems to be as good an idea as rumored. They romp and bowl one another over as we hike the trail to the Grass Dam and play hide and seek down the hill toward the jetties, surprising and tackling each other into the gentle arms of the long dry grass. They were two passed out puppies, sleeping peacefully for almost an hour until David called up to me that hornets were invading the basement where he was straightening cane. Sounded fascinating to them! Twice the excitement.

I've put my rod on hold until we get a better handle on them. They stick closer to us in the woods than Kodiak did, but demand more attention now than he did these past years. As a pup, maybe not so. I seem to remember wrestling on the bed with him to allow David time for his graduate work in hydrology, Kodiak, a high-energy pup who unraveled both the arms of my sweatshirt thread by thread over the course of our romping. They haven't taken his place, but they are creating a new place of their own, as we'd been told they would. Good advice from Jerry - once you've loved dogs, you have to fill that space. Good advice from Tom - get them both. Mostly, they keep us too happy and too busy to think about it.

Saturday, October 9

*B*eautiful fall day. It actually is, despite a somewhat shaky start. Effie had barked us to consciousness just after midnight. She'd made a substantial mess on the puppy newspaper, then dribbled all across the floor. My turn, so I took her out after flushing the evidence, and she had miserable results. I'd no more settled us all back to sleep when she whined again, and David took her out with a similar outcome. Midge, though groggy, just looked for stones. Mouthing and chewing stones have suddenly become important to both pups.

The third time she cried, Effie just wanted to cuddle, so I passed two hours dozing with her on my lap. Then we were up and out again. David took the next turn while we both shook the sleep out of our thoughts and settled on the problem. Chewing stones, miserable. Teething, maybe? I poured some water on their dry food and we decided to monitor them on a walk. In truth, only David and I walked; the pups were all energy and romping. They were still playing while I read the puppy first aid book, no food for twenty-four hours with loose stools. Blew that already.

It's a good day when everything is both interesting and works out in the end.

We drove up to the mountains to celebrate Barb's birthday and to deliver some donations for the Casting for Recovery auction, a benefit that combines fly fishing and women recovering from cancer. There's a dusting of snow at the ski resort and across the craggy peaks of Bigelow and the ridge that is the long summit of Abraham. What color still clings to the trees in the valleys gives way to the dark firs and spruces of the mountainside. We detoured to a sheltered pond, just to check: moose, yes.

Fires are glowing in both woodstoves for the first time tonight. David is working on cane, the sweet scent of heated bamboo drifting upstairs. Effie and Midge fit easily on one dog bed in front of the woodstove, barely awake enough to chew on their toys but reluctant to give way to sleep. My turn to keep an eye on them. I took them out for a moment, thinking maybe they'd sleep if we finished that detail of the evening. The wood smoke was mixed with autumn night, no moon, starlight muted by invisible clouds so the geese are staying tight on the pond. I could just see the silver wake of the otter swimming, diving, leaving great circles like the trout of favorite dreams. We found it on land yesterday, rustling in the fallen leaves and across the carpet of spent yellow needles below the sheltering white pines, then pausing to watch us watch it before sliding into the water. The puppies were oblivious; there were too many shoreline sniffs.

In front of the warm stove, Midge and Effie have traded places on the dog bed, still clinging to the evening, pausing to cuddle, get a drink, then chewing again. Effie is just starting to show little Midge her chew bone. Midge will eventually bite, pouncing her. Then they'll chase each other around the house until it escalates too much. They'll both lose control as the evening progresses, the game of tag that'll last until they pass out to sleep.

Changing Planes

Tuesday, October 12

Atlantic salmon keep leaping into my life. Whoever dubbed them the "Fish of Kings" must have been having a tough day on the water or, more likely, was contemplating a trip to a name brand lodge for a chance at bragging rights and caught instead a glimpse of the price tag. In my world they've become a symbol of an exciting, wild, native fish which is all together real, accessible, and in need of immediate and direct help. Whether or not I ever catch another one remains to be seen; whether or not I ever fish for Atlantic salmon on purpose also remains to be seen. But as a close neighbor in need, our paths are increasingly intertwined.

At last night's Trout Unlimited meeting, our guest was Dan McCaw of the Maine Atlantic Salmon Commission. His plea for help was as frustrating to me as it was interesting, frustrating because I realized that I didn't know half of the initialisms being tossed about, interesting because he needed help with a project to incubate Atlantic salmon eggs streamside in the mountain headwaters of the Kennebec.

"'This is Dan McCaw with the ASC, hoping we can help out with a MOU for AS eggs from Craig." Greg Ponte introduced the young man in uniform. I could see that the ASC must be a Maine Agency – there was a patch of the State of Maine on his green coat – and I knew enough to realize that Craig probably wasn't a person with an interesting stash of little salmon but the big hatchery near Bangor at Craig Brook. In fact,

Kathy Scott

I had met Dan's counterpart, Paul Christman, somewhere maybe in the park with an Atlantic salmon display one May on the Kennebec?

Dan was polite, down to earth, and down to business.

"Thanks for having me here tonight, and thanks for your interest in our project. Greg tells me that he thinks you might be willing to help us out."

He went on to explain that Paul, his boss, had initiated a project incubating eggs of Atlantic salmon up toward Rangeley in a headwaters stream of the Kennebec. The idea was that the fry would imprint on those waters and return, hopefully, about the time that upstream passage became available. Avon Stream ran down from Mount Blue to the Sandy River and on to a confluence with the Kennebec, then out through Merrymeeting Bay to the ocean. It was traditionally an Atlantic salmon river, but dams and interruptions in the runs of alewives were among the many and often unknown reasons that the fish had all but disappeared. Still, north of Edwards, Dan explained, the ES designation didn't apply. Across the table, Jimmy Thibodeau, who fishes the Kennebec every day of the season, knew of rumored Atlantics caught by accident just below the last dam, one or two a year, maybe, but it was anyone's guess if there were more.

The Big Picture wasn't the topic for discussion, though. Paul and Dan needed help this year with streamside incubators made from old refrigerators outfitted as a filtering tank and a safe shelter for the hard to get eggs. They needed a partner which could offer volunteer labor to check on the system throughout most of the winter, digging up the tanks if the snow was deep to check whether the water was flowing or frozen in the lines, or shoveling snow onto the system if we had an open winter and insulation was needed against the cold. Especially during runoff in the spring, a major change in stream flow could eject the intake hose from the stream. Suddenly freed ice could press up on to the bank and move the tanks out of level or worse. It was a long drive to the site and it would be cold, not a project for the faint of heart. The only rewards would be an opportunity to test this type of experimental system, which could work for brook trout restoration in a stream where the gravels had been displaced but where trout would otherwise live, and a slim chance to help an unknown population of Atlantics regain a foothold back in their native waters.

We wanted in. Greg would coordinate our efforts and write the MOU, which turned out to be a legal document, a memorandum of understanding, one step beyond a gentleman's agreement but not quite so binding as a contract. We were committed, no doubt, but I was guessing there were some uncertain factors on the other side, not that I was totally sure who the "other side" was.

The rest of the meeting was interesting, as always, but two parts stood out to me. Jeff Reardon, our regional Trout Unlimited coordinator, thought he'd found two Atlantic salmon redds in another tributary of the Kennebec and would be leading anyone interested to look them over on Saturday. David and I volunteered. Then, sometime between my musings over that outing and my awe for the selfless work done by the people around the table, my name landed at the head of the officers' slate for a vote at the next month's general meeting.

Kathy Scott

Caught.

A wave of realization swept through me, choices ahead. Where did my priorities lie? To wrangle the stuff of life like repairs and maintenance, train and exercise two adopted puppies, and finish my rod, or to do my part taking a turn, ready or not? I stifled a laugh at my private cliches, relieved no one else could hear my thoughts: if not me, who? if not now, when? Logically, no one has time for things like being the president of an active Trout Unlimited chapter, but there was no way I could protest after hearing earnest promises of support I knew would be kept. I also realized it meant that I had some homework ahead.

Tonight I'm researching the history of Atlantic salmon in Maine, the life cycle stages, and a host of acronyms. Our friend Carl Cote, another director, has volunteered to make a list of the state-related acronyms for use by those of us lost at meetings, but I need a few now. The Atlantic Salmon Commission is actually part of Maine government, not to be confused with the ASF, the Atlantic Salmon Federation, a conservation group like Trout Unlimited in many ways. The Maine Chapter of the ASF seems largely to be members of the Atlantic salmon clubs, like the ones formed around the past spectacular fishing in the pools of the Penobscot, the next major watershed east of the Kennebec. Fishing has been closed on the Penobscot only since the 1980's when the Atlantic salmon was declared endangered in Maine. ES, endangered species. At that time, the Edwards Dam on the Kennebec near Augusta marked the northern limit to fish passage in the system, so the ES designation wasn't continued upriver or into the tributaries. If it had been, there's a good chance the recovery project Paul and Dan were attempting wouldn't have been allowed.

Just so I can speak salmon fluently, on Saturday while wading the river (the Sheepscot, it turned out) looking for redds, I thought it best to find out what a redd actually is, what it looks like. I knew it was essentially a bed where the female lays the eggs; I didn't realize that it could be quite long and was characterized by brighter gravel (from her moving it) and two major parts: the long freshly covered hole where she excavated the gravel and laid the eggs and the hole adjacent and upstream where she excavated more gravel to cover the eggs. About eight feet of bright gravel, sign of an Atlantic salmon redd.

Then eggs develop into eyed-eggs, which hatch into sac fry, also called alevin (I like that), little fish with a yoke sac on their tummies, sometime late in spring. After three weeks or so, keyed by water temperature, the sac is absorbed and the fry find their way up out of the gravel of the redd. The fry grow into the parr, sides barred and darting about in the safety of their natal stream for about three years, maybe long enough for the Kennebec to allow passage, but maybe with luck high enough water, at least, so they can safely pass through the gauntlet of dams. Somehow, the chemistry of the parr changes as they migrate down toward saltwater. Then, the salmon babies are smolt, ready for a life at sea for maybe three years, until something deep inside calls them back toward the stream of their birth. If the smolt don't make it to salt, they desmolt and try it again the next year, with any luck. At most, a total of six years. Will that be enough to move the powers that be to provide for a safe trip upstream?

Kathy Scott

The Sandy River flows near our house, about six miles away on the other side of Mercer, not that there is much now to mark Mercer-proper, a few houses, a town office building by the old mill turned library. The stream that fed the mill in historic times was fed in turn by the stream out our window, Hilton Brook. It's interesting to think of Allen Hilton, selectman of Mercer in 1922, and his wife, unnamed in local records except as the daughter of an 1880's cobbler and cooper. At what point in their lineage did wild salmon return to Mercer to lay their eggs? Could they walk along the stream that bears their name, the stream we walk daily, and see brightly graveled redds? There is a dam on the Sandy now, an obstacle for anadromous fish (fish which live in the sea but breed in fresh water). Greg says there is talk of removing it, negotiations that may need a hand with removal costs later on this year. Maybe a TU chapter Embrace-A-Stream grant, something for the agenda as soon as they elect the next president.

"David," I asked tonight, "Does it sound lame to say 'If not me, who? If not now, when'?"

"Who cares if it does?" he grinned back.

Changing Planes

Thursday, October 14

We had to hide the fake stone with the compartment for the spare keys. Effie and Midge discovered it, and the keys were temporarily lost in the stone wall while they celebrated a new rock to chew. We're not wild about their obsession with stones, but their vet seemed to think that big stones and little stones were of no real concern. On our morning walk to the Grass Dam, they decided that hardened coyote scat was as good as a rock toy, and I had to take it away, embedded little bones and all. Unfortunately, it gets softer in a puppy's mouth. This evening, on the east jetty, Midge rolled in something musky, so we did baths for two.

Their first journey north to the brook was in between. They followed close at my heals, waded tentatively in the stream, and led all the way back with only a couple of corrections. Midge was worried about the splash a stone makes in the water. She ran back up the bank to watch from a safe distance, head cocked and ears up, peeking from behind a knee-high fir. Effie, the worrier, didn't worry at all. You never know.

Kathy Scott

Saturday, October 16

A gentle evening rain, an autumn rain, continued on from this morning. I was still able to walk the pups, although Midge ate coyote scat again. She wanted to kiss me afterwards to apologize. No! We saw a single goose swimming on the pond, calling. Just one and apparently lonely.

The pups tore through piles of leaves while I loaded firewood into a small wagon, three trips from the pile to the basement door. They kept close, to my relief, and followed me inside to watch with fascination the great alchemy that will be tomorrow's chili and cornbread. I cut and sliced while they learned that the stubs of carrots for teething are all they get of human food. Venison (deer meat in literal, say it like it is, Maine), corn, tomatoes, and three kinds of beans are for the humans in the house.

"Watch this while you can," I told them, "its pretty rare that I'd be cooking."

David, meanwhile, has been beveling strips of cane. He heat-treated some earlier, in between running errands with the pups in the car. We're trying to get them used to riding before any big trips come up; Midge has trouble keeping food down on the road. Just like switching them from the kitchen to the bedroom coaxed them to sleep through the night, switching from the truck to the car seems to have turned the corner on their riding. Now they just sleep.

Changing Planes

There's a crescent moon tonight, a small beacon, though still bright enough to light the way for the geese to find safe haven here before the hour gets late. The Big Dipper is fully upright. It'll be joined soon by a host of stars with enough cold starlight to keep the geese from getting too nervous. For now, they mumble and occasionally warn each other as they cross territories on the pond.

The pups are teething again, canines, and can't get comfortable. They've worked dental chews to nubbins already and have had enough treats for one evening, even sharing tough pretzels with David. Good pups, they whine just a little tonight and only occasionally. They were crabby earlier today, so tired from being miserable that they escalated their play to a near squabble down by the Grass Dam. We finally had to carry them back. Pooped pups. Effie has continued climbing into my chair with me; Midge has claimed her own chair right next to David's. When Effie's teeth hurt too much, I sit with her on my lap and rub her gums while David strokes Midge's ears so she won't be jealous. Now the pups are cuddled on a dog bed together, just in front of the woodstove.

Tuesday, October 19

Instead of waiting the extra two hours for David, I left right after work for an early romp with the waiting pups. The thought was that more exercise would make them sleep better. They were wound up. With a little growth spurt keeping them off kilter, I was clipped twice by puppy shoulders as they raced by, banking too sharply. I bribed them with puppy treats, luring them back to the house for supper and a sandwich for myself, then David joined us for a walk to the Grass Dam. The pups stretched out and ran, a joy to see, but disappeared on the return trip. Then Midge tore past flaunting a prize with Effie in pursuit. A stick? It smelled like a muck-extracted one, if it was. Our Midgey, cute as a button and into the earthier side of life.

We spent a frustrating eternity trying to catch her on a pass-by as she raced back and forth beneath the pines until I finally lured her using Effie as bait. I nabbed Midge; David took her smelly prize. What was it? A freshwater clam?

"Nope," he identified it, "a old, rotten goose's head."

Nice.

We bathed them both, and their pup-play escalated as they dried in front of the woodstove until Midge thought she was hurt, and Effie didn't know what happened, so David put his foot down. Then they slept. They are so cute sleeping that it's easy to forgive them any of the trials of youth, although we have discussed how we were going to juggle their futures and still get something accomplished. We scheduled their spaying for the day before Thanksgiving so we could be with them at the vet's and on through the holiday. As for cane, since David has a list of anglers waiting, and I have only trout streams waiting, I don't mind deferring most of my free time to the pups for now, giving him some time for rod work.

Changing Planes

Kathy Scott

I have not found the answers, though
I believe in partial and fragmentary ways
they have begun to come to me.

~ Wendall Berry

Changing Planes

Thursday, October 28

$\mathcal{A}$ beautiful full moon again tonight. Last night the clouds parted just as the total eclipse began, incredible luck to see it. Tonight luck of another kind, simple peace on Earth. Effie and Midge are sitting on either side of me watching David plane the butt strips of Steve's rod to their final dimension. He finished three of Jeff's, too; maybe we'll glue Saturday night. Two new rods for two new friends.

Voices of geese are drifting up from the pond. They come in, rest, and continue on, replaced by a new flock which does the same. I wait each evening to hear them in the distance, to listen to the water sounds of their coming in, and hope to be listening when the excited chorus grows in the morning, Canada geese finding each other, taking flight together. A solitary goose, an oddity in a species which mates for life, has appeared at strange times in strange places these last few days. I wonder each time if it will go along.

Tuesday, November 2

A heavy mist is falling that is probably snow in the mountains. Dark comes early with the time change, although the pups are easier to see these days. Their coloring, long brown, tan, and black plumes, makes them nearly invisible all autumn, but the orange bandanas of November show up well in low light. They are looking more like golden retrievers crossed with border collies, but I think there are the genes of cuddly, plush stuffed animals in there, too. They love to snuggle.

David pulled the string off the bound butts we glued, then rebound them. He had a rendezvous in town today with Bill from Labrador, Annie's uncle's rod in hand. It was an H. L. Leonard, the rodmaking company beginning with that maker's own name in Bangor just after the Civil War then migrating to the Catskills in New York. This was a model 50 DF, an 8-foot, 3-piece, 5-weight with two tips, one of them delaminating. More than that, it was a symbol of a new friendship, a trust in the recognition of a kindred respect for some basic things that are worth preserving. What paths do people take that they should have crossed as ours did?

They crossed deliberately at noon in Mike and Linda's shop, often suspected as the center of the Universe. Bill had insisted on giving us the rod; David advised him of its potential value and refused. In the end, they compromised and met half way, both convinced of the good to be found in the world. We'll keep the rod safe until it someday finds its way into the next caretaker's hands. Meanwhile, we'll fish it now and then for Annie's uncle.

The pups are sleeping. I'm smiling; I searched tonight but never found the lone goose. Now, though, I can hear more coming in. Lovely.

Saturday, November 6

David needed time to work on tip strips, so I walked the pups this afternoon, a Big Walk. I stopped by the south house to find more coats against the chill, including my blaze orange vest. The pups were sporting their matching collars. With binoculars, David might be able to spot us from the deck most of the afternoon.

Midge and Effie bowled each other over, crouch and attack, border collie style, all across the clearing and down the hill, just beating me to the Grass Dam. Twelve inches of snow blanketed the mountains last night, and my nose welcomed the cold air. It had fallen as rain for us, though, and the pond was swollen and overflowing the dam. The pups were just as happy not to cross it, so I taught them a new path.

We retraced our route back as far as the cutoff to the Big Rock, arriving there at roughly the same time. They lapsed into their good pup behavior, following me closely after that through hummocks of grass toward the north. New territory for them. We flushed a hen and a drake black duck, but that was it.

Kathy Scott

We paused just long enough at the north house for me to admire David's work, then continued north along the brook. Eight ring neck ducks, usually tame but skittish while migrating, flew off and to the south. We watched them fly, and then turned back north to a sight I'd hoped not to see. A single goose was in the northeast marsh, just ahead. It moved along the North Dam, then seemed to shuffle over it. The goose was so far away and the grasses were so long, I couldn't tell much of anything. Was this the same goose? Was it hurt? The questions had begun to plague me. If this was the same goose, was it wounded, or was it just heartbroken and lingering over a lifelong mate now lost? I'd hoped the lone goose was gone; I could feel my own heart breaking.

I radioed David.

"There's a lone goose in the brook just beyond the north dam," I told him.

"Well, Don is here at the house, and says he'd like to meet the girls," he replied, not the answer I expected, but, then, I didn't know what to expect as far as the goose was concerned. Don was Don Taylor, recently retired from a career with the Maine Department of Inland Fisheries and Wildlife, known locally as The Department. Maybe he'd have some ideas.

Wouldn't hurt to show off the pups, too, I smiled to myself. The Girls. They were being so good.

After some coffee, talk, and puppy greetings, we three decided to walk Effie and Midge to the north again, and try to better examine the goose while discussing what should and could be done. This was new ground for us, Canada goose tending. Was a migratory bird even ours to tend? Certainly, there was a strong case for nature taking its course. On the other hand, by allowing hunting, hadn't we also made a pact with the animals involved? Probably, but what was it?

We brainstormed along the marsh with Don. If we found it, and if it was wounded, what then? Might it freeze or starve, or could there be enough time before freeze-up for it to heal? If there was no future but a slow death, should we call The Department and allow it to be shot? Would they allow it to be shot with hunting season over? Should we just take care of it quietly? At what point? Would we?

Don had come by to see the pups, not wade, so he wasn't wearing boots. Neither was David. We couldn't find the goose again - it might have flown - before the water blocked our way northward. We worked our way south again along the shore of the pond. Effie and Midge were eager to visit ground they'd just learned and led the way. We hadn't gone far when they started to bark. The pups seemed to think there was something across the pond. We three humans looked in vain for a moose until someone's gaze fell closer. Floating only a few feet from shore, a goose, partially submerged, a beautiful bird. That could mean that the other one was lingering to be near it. A forlorn mate, maybe? Hundreds of geese come through; by sheer numbers we knew some must in all likelihood die here, witness the pups' prize a few days before. Maybe this goose was totally unrelated to the other, another migrant. But if not, maybe burying this one would free the other to join a flock one of these nights and fly on. Who could resist their excited liftoff each morning? We'd almost flown south, just to be a part of it.

We made our way back to the yard with Don, but the pups had disappeared. They burst into the clearing suddenly, Effie in the lead. Don and David grabbed Midge, in pursuit but close enough to nab. Effie obviously had a prize Midge wanted. I found a way to position myself on a pass-by when she was flaunting her treasure toward Midge and Don, and made the interception. The smelly toy again. She gave it to Don.

"Good girl," he told her.

Tuesday, November 9th

All light is low light in November. Today marked the pups' first trip all the way around the ponds. They looked even more beautiful enriched by the long rays as they passed the place where David and I had buried the goose. I was testing to see if the pups might detect the buried goose and maybe be tempted to dig it up. No. Not to anthropomorphize, but trying to achieve an appropriate balance, all things considered, we'd laid it deep in the earth along the shore and wished it well. That didn't seem to come out right, but I continued, anyway, whispering off to the north.

"There's nothing more you can do," I pleaded with the lone goose, nowhere to be seen or to hear me. "Go south."

The pups and I continued north, where I realized that the ice was more extensive than I had thought. At twenty-one degrees, the approaching winter had glazed most of the still water. The pups ran to a favorite drinking spot and stopped cold.

Changing Planes

They seemed surprised, but I meant to surprise them more. Even if David had been along, I'd rather have them avoid the ice entirely, so I had no intention of letting them be comfortable on thin ice with only me there to save them. I stepped between the pups and crashed a hole through the frozen surface with my foot, scaring them. Then I tested the effect by trying to coax them back for a drink, but they seemed to get the point. Even so, we followed a route that kept them well back from the water.

Once we were past the northeast marsh, I breathed a little easier. Far less chance of an ice disaster there. I started us out in this direction because I wanted to look for the lone goose, hopefully winging its way south. Otherwise, I wished either I wouldn't find it or, if I did, there would be a clear course of action apparent. At our Trout Unlimited meeting last night, I'd asked around for advice, what if? "It's a hard thing," they said, and divided into two groups. Call a wildlife rehabilitator, someone who could teach you how to save it. Let nature take its course; some of our Canada geese are wild migrants, some are up from southern New England, some are residents, but it adds up to too many for the habitat to support.

Underlying apparently opposing opinions, there is always a greater truth. When one of my students was about to take his first steps toward wading the tailwaters of the Shawmut Dam on the Kennebec, I advised him to just be straight with the other anglers there, many probably these same guys. "Be honest about being new, and they'll help you out," I'd explained. "Just ask them what flies to use and where to fish them. Tell them you're in the high school fly fishing club."

Kathy Scott

When he returned, he told me it went pretty well once he'd thought about their answers.

"The first angler told me 'you can't go wrong with flies on the surface.' The next guy I asked said to try a streamer as deep as I could get it to go. I was looking through my fly box when a third guy tells me 'the secret is to fish a wet fly half way down.' I decided the fishing must be good no matter what fly I picked. They were all right."

At the time, it reminded me of cane rodmakers advising each other about choice of glue for making rods, Urac, Epon, Resourcinol. There are as many right ways to apply the final finish: dip the rod in a tube of varnish, drip out the varnish, spray it on, brush it on. Finishes, more choices, all someone's favorite: spar urethane, varnish, Tru-oil. David has been conferring with Mike Brooks about the Payne finish, taking shellac flakes, an insect by-product, mixing them with alcohol, then diluting twenty-five per cent with lacquer thinner.

Life is full of right answers, choosing mine would be the trick. I had noted my conservation group's commitment to the salmon egg project and tried to reconcile two thoughts in my head, endangered species restoration and overpopulated species intervention, Atlantic salmon and Canada geese, but I was distracted from following up when the elections awarded me new immediate duties at the meeting, so the matter remained unresolved. If you can do something, should you?

The pups apparently think you should; they're always finding some new amusement. We were totally distracted with blackberry bushes when they found a five-point antler some buck had dropped. They found us our first shed moose antler; we've half-looked for one for years. Today, when I lingered too long, they discovered poopsicles filled with berries and seeds. Coyotes? I shooed them along and we headed to the brook. All along it, I kept one eye on the pups, the other looking for the goose. The uncertainty of the whole situation haunted me. Was it hurt? Was it even still around?

We hopped the stream and headed south back along the opposite side of the North Pond. The old beaver has had its work cut out trying to keep this pond dammed. The North Dam is so porous that water is easily seeping through. It looks like the center may give way, like the Big Dam's breech to create the jetties. When it goes, the Big Pond will become a stream, too, and the South Pond will be the only jewel left of the Hilton Brook necklace.

We crossed up and over the west jetty and continued to circle south. This was more new territory for the pups, so they stayed close. We followed packed moose and hare trails through the tamaracks. With my hat off, I could hear the pup's footfalls behind me. I kept a swift pace, hoping their intention to keep up would outweigh any urge to wander. In the long grasses that were once Bull Moose Cove, they had to struggle to stay close. I couldn't help but appreciate the gift of time, the change offered us in that very spot. Hidden but quite landbound in the long grasses was the very log which had once snagged Kodiak's collar when he fell through the ice, nearly drowning him one November. We walked over it.

Effie recognized the next well worn trail as the one on Hemlock Ridge. She claimed the lead, Midge following, then me. They didn't charge ahead, though, still respectful of their own inexperience. I practiced pointing out a direction change by saying "this way" at the fork down to the former Duck Cove, now mostly marshland, too.

At the Grass Dam, now huge thanks to its bold new resident beaver whose impressive food cache rose above the surface near the immense lodge, Midge followed me closely, conquering the crossing the first time. Effie tried every other alternative her puppy imagination could conceive before finally following. Then they both charged off, swerving to the north. They were through the trees and into the marsh before I could blink. I only caught up with them when they found yet another dead goose. With literally hundreds coming by, true wild geese from the north, not so wild opportunists from nearby states south, some expected mortality is the nature of life. Midge rolled on it; Effie grabbed a wing and ran. Puppy joie de'vivre. It was so decomposed it fell totally apart, dust to dust, the course of things. A coyote or a fox had been there, too, and mice or shrews.

I leashed the pups and started back, the last leg of the circuit. Although I saw it first, there was little I could do to distract the pups from seeing the six-point buck heading toward us on the path. I braced myself for the jolt from the leashes, but the pups showed no interest. Who would have thought?

The old beaver greeted me by swimming very near us as we paused below the north house. His trailing silver wake turned golden in the setting sunlight. As much as I care about him, I directed the pups up hill to dinner and bedtime. Later, when we took them out for the last time, the Northern lights were just starting, a green glow low to the north. Magnetic green fingers caressed the treetops. Maybe by midnight they'll reach the zenith.

Changing Planes

Saturday, November 20

The cold has deepened, all but the quickest water frozen fast. Most of it supports our weight easily. A light dusting of snow reveals all kinds of tracks the pups have followed all along, but that we've only suspected. Yesterday, we still found moving water immediately downstream of the dams and in the tiny rapids and pool by the east jetty. The pups and I stood there on the old beaver's scent post, and he appeared, a head in the water. It was well before dark, so the brilliant silver V of his travel wasn't there. The pups saw the head coming, but had no idea how to interpret it. I thought they might scare the old beaver off, but he tried to establish our identity by smacking his tail while only a few feet away. Effie's feathery tail tucked between her legs, and she raced back to the house. Midge, a little more curious, retreated over the berm of the jetty and peeked from a safe hideout on the other side, only her brown eyes showing. The old beaver and I laughed, or, at least, I did; it swam off to the other jetty and climbed ashore to nibble the bark on a small tree.

Kathy Scott

The same dear old beaver appeared in the same place tonight and swam over to see us. The pups sat behind me at a safe distance this time and watched. Free to resume my old relationship, I crooned "Here-beaver-here-beaver" as I used to do, and it swam closer. Although I'm not sure why, I've always wanted to touch this beaver. Maybe it's a symbol of a mutual trust I need, I don't know. With winter approaching, it seems unlikely to happen this year. I wish I could. This old beaver probably lived here long before it was our home, probably through other cycles of pond to stream to pond again. Would this pond come back again? Would this beaver be here to make it happen? Or would things just carry on without it, someday without me?

Loneliness tried to creep in while we shared the moment, me crouching on the ice, it hanging in the black water feet away. Not loneliness, that old feeling of nostalgia, of knowing there is something to be missed here, of trying to take it all in, immerse myself in it before it is gone. At the very least, enjoying the moment so that, one day, there is the quiet satisfaction of having loved it as best I can.

I blew a kiss toward the old grandfather beaver and stood up to gather the pups, but my smile faded. Just past Midge and Effie, perched on the top of the north dam, a lone goose was almost out of sight near the last free-flowing water.

"Why are you here?" I asked, aloud. "Oh, why are you here?"

I ran across the ice, a frozen shortcut, and found the goose again just as it slipped into the water. Odd white feathers made a strange angle at the tip of its left wing.

Saturday, December 4

Six inches of fresh, brilliant, fluffy snow fell last night, blanketing the ponds, the balsam fir, and the clearing in winter white. It was the stuff of which happy hearts are made, but I had one more thing to do before mine would be content.

The pups recovered so well after their surgery two weeks ago that it's been tough keeping them anything approaching the quiet the vet recommended. We'd walked them in short, well-controlled jaunts around the yard until we saw that the stitches held through an eruption of puppy play. Keeping them subdued became more stressful than letting them romp might be, so we were as glad as they were when the time for bed rest was over. This evening, though, I had them on leashes and headed north. I needed their help.

Once the lone goose was established as living near the ice shelf along the last open water of the brook, just over the dam, we found it daily. Sometimes it would already be swimming around the small flowing pool, sometimes hurrying back from the secretive marsh grasses as we approached. As the ice closed the pool more and more, the goose no longer felt safe in the water, but would pull itself up onto the shelf of sheltered ice on the far side and huddle down, its back to us. We kept our distance, wanting only to monitor it, not to add stress to its marginal existence.

With the new found familiarity grew a personal need to act. We still had no idea what was the right thing to do or what the possible courses of action might be, but exploring our options seemed uninvasive. What could that hurt? I searched about for wild animal rescue facilities and called most on my list. The story was the same: we don't work with wild geese, but it might be fine anyway if it finds food (apparently over-wintering wouldn't be a concern). Honestly concerned but overburdened volunteers told us that they were retired and too old to chase geese in winter, maybe we could catch it if we made a trap, baited with corn. Often, they had full cages already. Everyone had another number to call, but, in the end, there weren't any real options there.

I don't know why it took us so long to call the warden's service. Yesterday, Friday, we talked to a dispatcher after work, and the warden arrived from a situation farther north just before dark. It wasn't until she was on the way across the pond with us that we discovered that she was a neighbor, Cheryl Barton, the wife of a famous maker of wood fired brick ovens, Albee Barton, someone for whom David had repaired a cane rod. Small interesting world.

"Don't worry," she told us, watching the goose. Then she explained. "You'd probably never catch this one with a cage, the area is too open. It's going to be too dark to do it tonight, but tomorrow I'll bring my Labrador retriever and another warden. The dog has a very gentle mouth and he can out run this goose. He's helped us out before."

We found our way back to her truck by moonlight.

"After you catch it, then what?" we asked.

Cheryl said they'd transport the goose to live out its days in a facility down state.

We had trouble sleeping last night. In trying to do the right thing, maybe we'd done something very wrong. Were our intentions really so pure, so centered on the goose, or were we just trying to fulfill some need of our own? Call it guilt, call it misplaced empathy, it didn't matter. That need to do something may have been more of an end than a means. What kind of life would a wild Canada goose really have in such a place? Close quarters with other birds, unable to fly, to flee, to claim its territory. No matter how good the place, it wouldn't be life in the wild. It would die there eventually, no matter what life it had, and disease might well find it. Was this new life preferable to a slow northern winter death? Maybe.

Kathy Scott

The snow began drifting in around midnight, so we were forced to leave in the wee hours for a commitment we couldn't break or even postpone. We wanted to be home when the wardens and dog came; we couldn't be. As soon as we returned and shoveled the doorways clear, we called. There were no tracks; maybe they didn't even come out in the storm. I could tell that was exactly what I was hoping as I dialed.

Yes, they had come out just after dawn, the warden explained, but she had bad news. There was no goose. All signs pointed to a scuffle on the ice shelf, probably coyote. Then she explained how quickly coyotes work in these situations.

"The goose might never have known it happened," she said. "One minute it was asleep, the next it helped a coyote through a cold night."

I thanked her and set the phone down.

"Cheryl and the other warden brought the dog," I told David. "The goose was just gone, probably a coyote. She said it was probably quick." We both knew instantly that it was exactly the right solution.

"I just didn't feel right about the captivity idea," David said.

I could tell I agreed. I felt nearly complete relief. There would always be a tiny shred of wonder, of doubt - was there a coyote? - but that's how these things go. I looked out the big windows toward the snow-covered pond, brilliant white and pure.

"I'll make the fires if you want to walk the pups," David offered. Deal. I knew where we'd go, too.

The pups and I hurried north until we dropped over the frozen dam near the remnants of the last pool of flowing water, the goose's home. Across from us, blanketed, was the small shelf of ice where it had huddled out of the wind, and behind that the sheltering thicket of dense balsam fir, nearly black in contrast to the snow.

"Let's go around," I told the pups.

We found a safe spot to cross the ice, then stepped down tentatively onto the small snow-covered shelf, testing to see if it would support our weight. Yes. I brushed back the snow to clear the original shelf, then crouched down and pointed to the ice.

"Goose," I said, tapping the ice. Ever curious and agreeable, the pups sniffed the ice. Their tails went up. Goose!

I stood while their excitement grew, wrapping the ends of their leashes securely around my mittened hands, right for Effie, stronger, left for Midge, more eager to please. Time to grow up puppies, and show your stuff.

"Where's the goose?" I asked, making it sound as much like an exciting game as I could. "Where is it? Go!"

This was, of course, ridiculous, a probable product of reading too many dog stories as a child, but it worked anyway. The pups bounded through the deep snow, pulling me through the firs and out the other side. As we lumbered on through deeper snow in the low light toward the pines, I thought I could see a trough in the snow. They seemed to be following it.

Kathy Scott

The big white pines had caught and held much of the snowfall in their highest branches, so there was little beneath. Just enough for tracking. Even a human could see the trail now. We had followed the trough to the pines where it became canid tracks straddling something larger, something dragging.

A fallen pine had allowed enough light to grow a dense thicket of poplars, and the pups wanted to drag me inside. I hesitated, not sure if we really wanted to fight a coyote over its meal right then. Or ever. Scouting seemed in order while I gathered up my nerve. We circled around to the other side of the thicket where we saw two telling signs: there was a bit of blood on the snow; there were canid tracks leading out of the thicket, fresh, I thought. The pups were very interested in following. Instead, I directed them into the thicket. There we found a few remains, mostly feathers, odds and ends, a meal well devoured. I took one feather.

On the way back home, in a comforting twilight, I tied the pups to a fir, just for a minute. Then I crept cautiously to the edge of the shelf of ice and gently placed the feather on the water.

Changing Planes

Kathy Scott

Attentiveness cannot be kept casually,
or visited only in season...
The patterns of our lives reveal us.
Our habits measure us.

~ Mary Oliver

Changing Planes

Saturday, April 23

Time flies when you're having fun, accepted as fact. Time also flies when you're having snow, and this winter saw a mountain of it. Six inches fell the early December day that Effie and Midge graduated from being puppies to the more focused, wiser 'pups' level by helping discover the fate of the lone goose. Twelve inches fell the next day, and later, in two storms a week apart, twice twenty inches. Just when we thought we had that under control, twenty-three. I kept the yardstick near the snow shovel, both futile tools in the end.

It was a love-hate situation. We embraced the wonder, the sheer power such a lovely force can have to halt the world. Our world, anyway. We prioritized clearing the driveways, eventually sticking to just the north house driveway and donning snowshoes to travel to the south house and most everywhere else around home. Freeing the mailbox took on a life of its own; I spent hours with the shovel trying to sculpt a smooth approach for the carrier. Our walkways were of such low priority that we used clearing them only to fill a rare empty hour.

At the height of it all, the snow blower conspired against David, throwing him left, right, and, finally down. He landed in bed and miserable. Rod work was out of the question. None for him meant I certainly wasn't going to try to work on my rod, rubbing salt in the wound. I knew he wouldn't mind, but it just didn't seem right. Or smart. My confidence level was roughly equal to the pressure I felt to finish it.

It was our turn to tend the incubators for the Atlantic salmon eggs, though, and we decided that I should go. The project held great importance to both of us, and David thought it would be too much fun for me to have to miss it. Effie and Midge would stay home and keep him company, and I would drive out our narrow chute to the main road and on up to the headwaters stream in the mountains. I pulled on enough layers of clothing to guard against the cold, waterproof to allow wallowing in snow, and neoprene gloves for cold-water work. I tossed in the snowshoes.

The partnership is working out well. David's and mine, true, but also the partnership between the Atlantic Salmon Commission and Trout Unlimited. Greg had been the driving force in the liaison, bringing the ASC to our directors' meeting, and he continued to coordinate our efforts. He assisted Paul and Dan in readying the incubators and placing them streamside, and they had refreshed him in the steps necessary to assure the viability of the Atlantic salmon eggs throughout the winter, run-off, and spring. Greg had arranged the schedule of Kennebec TU volunteers, also training Craig Denis from the upriver Somerset TU. Craig would be training Mike and Linda from our TU with me today; we'd go back on our own when we could.

If I was an Atlantic salmon, or a brook trout for that matter, I couldn't think of a more beautiful place to be born. David and I had visited Avon Stream before the snows, a small mountain brook cascading over moss and boulders through gravel pools to the Sandy River. The Sandy is misnamed at its headwaters. It only stretches to a wider, gentler flow through sand as it passes down the valley to Farmington and on through

New Sharon. In Mercer, the rocky rapids have been silenced for decades by a small power dam, now virtually unused and begging to be removed. If it was, the salmon smolt would have a clear run all the way to the Kennebec. The thought was exciting. Difficult to achieve, maybe, but why not try? Already we were in lockstep with the dam owners, the landowners, and the State toward a joint effort to remove it.

Towering snow banks along the mountain road forced Linda and Mike, Craig, and me to park down and across from the stream. We waited to pull on snowshoes until we scaled the bank near an empty trailer, a vacation home of the absentee landowner who had graciously allowed us access. We crossed the clearing in single file, enjoying the exertion against the chill. The air wasn't cold by winter standards, but we all knew we'd be working in water shortly. Best to get warmed up now.

The steps down the bank from the clearing to the streamside were buried under mounds of snow; it was hard to say how many feet there were. Six steps? At the work site, the reclining refrigerators turned filter and incubator were buried as well. We used a probe to find them, then shoveled away two feet of new snow. With mittened hands, I swept back the last of the it to reveal the large white rectangle that was the door. It made an even white surface with the snow all around us.

What next?

Craig said that we'd open it up to confirm that water was flowing; if not, we'd be digging up the line from upstream to find where it was blocked by ice. If it was flowing, we'd still need to dig out the supply valve and shut off the flow while we changed the battens that capture the sediment in this tank before the water flows on to the tank holding the eggs. We'd also need to check that the water was flowing freely around the eggs, not frozen in the line, not frozen in the tank.

We pitched in. Mike started digging to find the valve near the side of the tank while Craig swung open the door. The water appeared to be flowing in slowly, as it should, a small trickle sheeting down over the vertical Plexiglas divider that separated the main tank from the standpipe battens and exit pipe. A D-shaped plastic manifold attached to the inlet. It was large enough to cover the bottom of most of the tank. Holes all along the manifold allowed the water to enter the tank; white matting trapped particles flowing in. When the water rises to the height of the divider, it falls over and fills the side compartments where five outlet standpipes, also made of perforated pvc wrapped with battens, screen sediments again before the flow exits through a tube under the snow and continues into the next tank. All of the white matting battens were an earthy brown.

Linda and I handled the replacement matting while Mike and Craig shut off the flow and cleaned out the tank. Craig retrieved the siphon hose from storage in a tree, and Mike tried his hand at siphoning the water out without getting too wet. He threatened to soak all of us, but resisted. Rocks held the batting that covered the manifold tight to the floor of the tank, so Mike reached into the icy water to retrieve them. As the battens were stripped from the outlet pipes, Linda cut new matting to size, and I wrapped them into place. The siphon hose was a nifty tool for sucking the last of the sediment off the floor of the tank. The flow across the divider was even, so we didn't have to dig down to wedge an outside corner or two of the tank to level it.

The work was cold with wasted moves extracting a human price, but we loved it. Freezing cold, wet, mucky work, and we actually considered ourselves rather sane. Whatever the outcome of this project, there was an underlying sense of importance in what we were doing, tangible effort toward elusive, untested results, but with a potential outcome that had captivated us. Would these eggs hatch? Would the young, any of them, pass down to the Sandy and on down through the four dams on the Kennebec unscathed? Would they ever find their way home?

That was weeks ago.

How did April come along so fast? Today was Saturday of the week-long April school vacation, the last Saturday of vacation, unfortunately. After a sunny spring week, a gentle rain fell today. David's sister joined us for a third jaunt into the mountains to tend the salmon eggs - much easier than in winter. David and I wore hip boots, and I wore neoprene gloves. We drained the tank, rinsed out the filtering battens in the stream (from whence came the sediment) and Barb repositioned them, securing the filters in place. A few eggs were white, dead, so we retrieved a turkey baster from the storage box to remove them before a fungus could grow and affect their siblings. The baster, unfortunately, was less than precise. We'd take in tiny live hatchlings, too. Fry. Salmon babies. Accepted biological names aside, from eyed-eggs to grisle, these would always be the salmon babies to me. We sorted the dead eggs by squirting a baster's contents into a little glass jar. With the eggs removed, I'd hold the swimming babies at eye level, giving them advice for their risky journey ahead.

"Good luck, little ones, travel safely. Wait for high water to sweep you over the dams, you don't want to mess with those turbines. Wait for the alewives to school in before you make that last run out to the sea; you can hide under the schools. Spend an extra year in the Davis Strait to buy us a little time. Why not? You'll like Greenland."

I wasn't sure of that, but white lies to fish must be okay. Barb tried to return my swimming audience to the tank, but I thought of one more thing.

"Oh! Wait until the shad migrate up the Kennebec to come back, they'll camouflage you. But do come back."

"They know this stuff," David assured me, but added his own good wishes; Barb, too. Couldn't hurt.

The way I see it, anthropomorphism is okay if mixed with a self-deprecating smile and the acceptance that many, maybe thousands, of these little fish would die, hard but part of the deal.

Also in the waterproof storage box I found the notebook of the project. Recorded in the log was my earlier trip with Craig, Mike, and Linda, and a later trip with David. Michael Jones, a free spirit, friend, and registered Maine guide, found the initial spring run-off had disrupted everything, throwing the intake hose out of the stream (it was now anchored to a tree). It had taken two days to right things again.

Changing Planes

  Even at home, the snow had exited rather dramatically - our dams had taken a beating. The North Dam and the Last Dam had finally both failed, draining the Big Pond to its historic streambed. The restored Grass Dam held, though.

  I had talked to Michael Jones later; he said that he had felt like Horton in the children's story, everything depending on him that day for hatching a Who. We all felt like that, I think. Hard not to feel protective. After him, the other Mike had returned without Linda to find the lack of snow allowed the hose to freeze, and he thawed it. Greg had several entries, as did the ASC biologists. Amazing to think they had done this all alone the year before, on top of their regular duties. We noted our work in the journal, too, then drove past a young moose to Rangeley for lunch. We continued across to Stratton the back way beneath Mount Abraham, then south past the Sugarloaf ski complex to the grocery store in Farmington and home.

  Spring fever took hold, and my planing form finally proved irresistible. The pups have settled into our lives or we've adapted to theirs, some compromise that works. I think I have a handle on my Trout Unlimited duties; the promises to provide any help I might need had great substance, as I knew they would. David was planing again.

  I set aside any fear of a last minute mistake and planed five of the tip strips to near final dimensions. David carried the heavy planing form I'd used up until now back to storage, a great form for larger rods than mine. We substituted one of the forms we'd purchased from their maker, Tony Larson, in Minnesota, and adjusted it to the dimensions for my tip. Tiny, tiny, tiny. I'd been warned about trying so diminutive a rod as this for my first. Still, a small stream rod would complement my five-weight nicely, a Garrison 193 and a Payne 97, tapers borrowed from Everett Garrison and Jim Payne, friends and collaborators, two men I never knew but admired. The warnings may just have egged me on a little, too.

I'd come to accept that the penalty for ruining a strip really isn't so severe, make a new strip, a few extra hours. Or set aside any false pride or dogma and actually ask for help, not hard for me to do, really, especially since the sixth tip strip concerned me right from the start. It had seemed a little different from the rest. The more familiar I became with it, the more it struck me as, well, different. An intuitive thing. Better to call in the Big Guns. David doctored the questionable strip to a healthy match with the others, carefully working a thin node to just exactly the final dimension. I watched and learned.

Sunday, April 24

The pouring rain began just after the pups and I returned from a brisk walk across the jetties and out through Bull Moose Cove. No incidents with other animals, although fresh moose tracks over ours gave me reason to leash the pups on the return trip. I released them to navigate the unsteady footing across the rocks, the miniature rapids of the jetties, and Midge rolled in an otter pile.

Changing Planes

Back at the shop, we tweaked the strips the last thousandth of an inch or so, just a little, then prepared for gluing. David rounded up the epoxy, brushes, scale, and odds and ends for the job while I laid out waxed paper and taped it to the countertop. He measured and I mixed the Epon glue, twenty grams of resin to eleven grams of hardener. With a thin blade, I sliced the masking tape holding the strips in a hexagonal imitation of their final place. Cutting each piece of tape at the apex between the same two strips allowed me to unroll them all and lay them flat, six strips closely side by side. I pulled on surgical gloves and dabbed a toothbrush in the tiny container of mixed epoxy, then carefully worked it along the length of the waiting strips, usually David's role. He took over my usual job, sighting along the strips from different angles to point out any places I missed with the glue.

Carefully lifting the butt ends first, I peeled the six strips off the waxed paper and rolled them together again. David checked them over, swabbing off excess glue with a paper towel while I held them hanging from the butt end. So far, so good. We moved to the binder.

There's something about binding that had me worried. Like my taper, our binder is also modeled after a design by Everett Garrison. The device is pretty ingenious - Garrison was brilliant - and it works well to spiral string around glued strips so uniformly that if a piece is trimmed off a well-crafted blank, it's impossible to see the six glue lines in the cross section. I knew that part worked. What concerned me was the way the tightly tensioned, weighted binder belt and string bent the blank while wrapping it. Those tiny tip ends suddenly seemed fragile, even though assisting on all of David's rods had shown me they weren't.

Kathy Scott

He'd never snapped one while binding the glued blank. My head said "go for it", my heart said "what if...". What worried me, too, was keeping the glued blank straight. More than once in classes or repeated tales, I knew of neophyte rodmakers baffled at the bend in their blanks; this was the key. The newly glued blank needed to be removed from the binder by lifting one end straight up without levering the other end against the binder. This step had grown in my mind to one of the most important in a straight, well-crafted rod, and I so wanted to do everything right.

We laid the taped, glued, soon-to-be blank in the curled supporting fingers of the binder. I pulled up a stool and took a breath. Then I wrapped the binder belt, a sturdy cord, around the cane, front to back, and tucked the end of the binding string through it, securing the string on the blank with a half-hitch. Then I turned the wheel and the string began to spiral along the length. I ran it up the rod to near the tip, paused, then asked for a demonstration. I chickened out.

Although it's usually better to bind continuously, my imagination and that tiny tip conspired against me. David ran the bound string up to the end of the tip, no problem, carefully lifted the cane off the binder without bending it, and tied off the string. Then he laid it back on the fingers in its initial position. I supplied vinegar and paper towels so he could clean the epoxy from his hands; then I wrapped the belt the other way, back to front, and repeated the process. I tied off the two ends of the binding string into a loop and found a safe place to hang the blank while the glue hardened. As we shared the cleanup, vinegar and paper towels, I practiced normal breathing.

Changing Planes

We finished the day with homemade chicken soup in front of the woodstove to chase away the dampness, followed by a nice evening walk. The jetties were bracing a roaring rapid, the brook filled with the all-day torrent. The morning flocks of blackbirds and the wood duck drakes flying after hens, the flickers, and the ravens left the night to the owls and coyotes, wood frogs clucking, spring peepers joining the chorus. The last patch of snow in the clearing melted today. Tonight, somewhere just north, a barred owl calls "who cooks for you?"

Thursday, June 6th

I looked at my blank today while wiping on another coat of Tru-oil. I've made over three hundred furled leaders since I glued it up and nursed my tennis elbow because of them. Donations to causes, mostly: supporting the effort of the Anglers of the Au Sable to defend its South Branch, donations to Casting for Recovery and various groups, banquets, fund raisers. Something good to be done matched with some little part I can play in helping. Hope I can cast soon, though.

Sanding the excess glue off my rod blank was probably where my elbow trouble really began. My doctor says he's never seen a case of tennis elbow that actually resulted from playing tennis. I waited far too long between gluing my strips together and removing the excess glue that had oozed out in the binding, cementing the string to the blank. I knew better, but I had set rod work aside while tending to other things, most of them self-imposed and some very dear.

To better understand our Atlantic salmon project, it seemed best to start at the beginning, their beginning. We drove one weekend to the Craig Brook National Fish Hatchery in East Orland, a beautiful facility with an interpretive center and an historic effort, only to discover that we wanted, needed, to explore the Green Lake National Hatchery near Ellsworth.

Craig Brook, the oldest public hatchery in the nation, has been raising Atlantic salmon to help replenish Maine rivers since 1871. Now it raises 1.5 million fry and smolt, housing broodstock from six rivers with endangered populations, but not our river. The eggs for our project come from Penobscot River salmon since Kennebec River eggs aren't available. To see their natal chambers, we drove to the spreading facility at Green Lake, seemingly deserted. We found our way in and located one lone attendant. At her invitation, we admired drawers and drawers of eggs in labeled racks, tanks and tanks of salmon of all sizes, the Dennys River strain visibly the most wary in their circular covered tanks.

The incubation project eggs were Green Lake Penobscots, she told us. No one had more than anecdotal evidence of the existence of Kennebec salmon. The few reported there might be Penobscot fish who'd wandered, who knew? We asked her about the Penobscot fish and the health of that river. She detailed how, from 500,000 returning adults in the days before dams, the population in the Penobscot decreased to a handful in the fifties. Only ten percent of the original habitat remained, and the return of other interrelated species to the river was dangerously low. This past year, the return of Atlantics to the Penobscot was around one thousand, stable since the fishing moratorium, but being the fish of choice for the aging angling population there, talk was escalating for a limited season, another thing I'd need to research.

And so on it went, all interesting.

Intertwining a rodmaking day here or later there, I attacked my hardened glue with the resolve demanded by a well-set space age epoxy, the added complication of attempting to remove excess glue as hard as rock. I needed to master the technique of preserving the corners of the hexagonal shape of the blank, the apexes, while sanding the flats down to cane. Wrapping 320 grit sandpaper on the small blocks David supplied, I laid the blank on my planing form and pulled on light gloves with the work side rubberized for a more certain grip. I substituted elbow grease for time, but it wasn't long before time and my elbows gave out.

Two flats into the work, I caved, appealing to David for help. There had to be another way. He showed me how to use the file to get a good start and then finish with the sandpaper. I experimented with holding the file flat, working it in one direction along a new flat, feeling, watching for that change in texture, brushing away the dust in hope of seeing the tortised brown of the blank appear. Before the end of the sanding, I surrendered in tears. My elbows didn't like the one-two sanding furling punch. David finished the last flats for me, and I submitted my elbow and bruised pride to the doctor, who prescribed rest and new crafts, and our angling friends, who prescribed appropriate exercises and arm support. I combined the rest with the exercises, and I resolved to plan my time better.

Since there's no chance that this rod could be finished and finished well for a trip to the stream this summer, I've decided to experiment with coating it with Tru-oil, fine for a rod on hold, but fine, too, in multiple layers for a ultimate finish. Jerry Kustich has used tung oil on his personal rods in the dry West, but David never has here in the East (David actually hasn't kept one of his own rods yet). Tung oil comes from a tree nut; Tru-oil is linseed oil based, another plant derivative. We reasoned that Tru-oil was used on gunstocks, which are used outdoors, and tung oil is used on furniture, which is mostly indoors. Fly rod, outdoors, Tru-oil. Agreeing that this seemed like a chance to experiment, David cut me a square of lint free cheesecloth, and I wiped some on, waited, and applied a second coat. The blank looks beautiful to me.

Saturday, August 7

Of one thing we'd been certain: Effie and Midge wouldn't like the long ride to Newfoundland any more than they'd like the black flies we'd found there. Instead, this summer progressed as an immersion in small trips, a greater exploration of the familiar adapted to explore this new role in our lives. Breadth and depth, that's this summer and last. If our exploration of the Maritimes celebrated the freedom to lay new paths, breadth, then our journeys this summer allowed us to see the details of the paths we've already traveled.

Things for us had changed, but changes just call for adaptations. The four-legged change loomed foremost. Kodiak had traveled well, had preferred the back of his truck to almost any place on earth. Last summer, for the first time in many, we'd traveled alone. This summer, two pups. While the jury wasn't in on their travel preferences, certain concessions would have to be negotiated; that was just part of the pledge we'd made. On the other hand, we knew that there was a real danger that Effie and Midge could dictate our direction just because they had so captured our hearts. While we would be watching for heat waves and alternate travel routes, steering toward dog-friendly places and activities, we began the summer with an amazing gesture thanks to David's sister and a college student turned dog sitter. For the first week, we left Effie and Midge with them and traveled alone.

There are a lot of anglers who shake their heads and wonder how we could have become fly fishers and remain pretty much oblivious to the storied past of the Catskill Mountains of New York. In retrospect, I can see their point. From the birth of the American dry fly to famous tyers like the Dettes and the Darbys, the storied Junction Pool and the anglers like Lee and Joan Wulff who wrote those stories, the little town of Roscoe, New York, has earned its place in fly fishing history. Still, when we were invited to join two other rodmakers for a team taught cane rodmaking class, we just thought it would be a good idea. We had no clue that we'd have within our grasp some of the best cane rods from throughout the ages. I had no idea that the sweet old elf who popped in to ask about furled leaders would be world renown for his Atlantic salmon flies until a fellow New Yorker, Art Port, whispered to me, my furling board in hand, "You do realize that's Poul Jorgensen?" I just thought that I'd found another kindred spirit, and I had. We learned fast, and by the time Ted Rogowski joined me for a Diet Coke on the tailgate of our pickup, it was nice to be able to thank one of the authors of the Clean Water Act in person.

This year, our second season, we knew better what to expect. By the third day of the class, the morning air was so intense and so hushed in the workshop we could hear the warblers' songs outside. With eight potential rodmakers and the four of us, David and I, Art, and Ron Barch, it would seem like the air would be filled with rod talk, but on day three, hands and minds are on planing strips, and that concentration is silent. Through the open doors, I could see a grazing cottontail, could almost hear it nibbling in the clover. The garden beauty of the place, the storied past, was mantled by the most serious work on earth.

But only for so long. As in our first class, hands and minds merged; kinesthetic memory slowly took over and began conquering any new-to-cane insecurity, just as it had done for me at home. Although everyone jumped when rodmaker-to-be Bob, a boat builder, broke the silence to ask if he could put on some music, not one of the students laughed, this was far too serious.

"Watch what happens," Ron whispered to David and me.

Bob pulled his car up between the cottontail and the open doors, lowered the windows, and slipped his Jimmy Buffet CD in the slot. In deference to the assumed variety of musical tastes in the room - the students ranged from a computer programmer to a hospital administrator to the local town doctor to our friend Carl, down from Maine - Bob kept the volume moderate, although we privately suspected that wasn't his usual way. The introduction and then the verse whispered around the room, pretty much matched by the long slow sliding sound of planes on steel. Eight separate blades shaved cane with increasing accuracy and finesse until each pass of the plane left a long blond curl. A foot here and a foot there tapped unconsciously to the music, shoulders relaxed, brows unfurled. On cue, the room came alive, voices spontaneously joining in.

"Wasted away again in Margaritaville, looking for my lost shaker of salt…"

Kathy Scott

We were never too serious again. Stories of fishing and fly rods, punctuated with laughter, with evolving nicknames, led to after hours hanging out on the bridge over the Willowemoc, sitting on tailgates with a scotch (or Diet Coke) and a cigar (not me). The music switched to Steve Goodman, to New York jazz, then to Ry Cooder. Details of rodmaking were examined, challenged, celebrated, and carried out. I took pictures of Ron in the shower showing Russ, aka Geppetto, how to quickly unglue a tip when one strip rolled over in the binding. David taught Mike the Brewmaster how to prepare the blank to receive a ferrule using a lathe. Art found a bandage for a nasty cane cut incurred by (hereafter known as) Mike the Finger, as opposed to Fishing Mike, who was in the stream every night. Doc Fried told us stories of Catskill days gone by, plans for the museum which lay ahead, and surgical instruments which are like rodmaking tools. Our meal breaks in the cool basement kitchen, from breakfast to last snacks, were full of the camaraderie which assures a reunion down the road, even among such divergent lives. Eight new rodmakers, eight new rods, under eight days.

Afterwards, we checked in on the pups, blissfully in love with their aunt and their sitter, then spent one last day apart from them, this time on the Kennebec River.

It was our first drift boat trip together. Our friend Sean insisted we three float the Kennebec, a river he knows well and that we love though rarely ever fish. It flows through our Trout Unlimited chapter and the towns where we work; our stream flows to the Sandy and then on into its waters. Sean was determined we fish, and David did. Wondering if I'd ever get it right, I suffered so from my over used elbow that I could barely

Changing Planes

cast a fly rod. Sean anchored near some rips, and we three waded to a likely spot. I was much relieved when David had a good sized trout on and averted Sean's gaze from me. I cast my dry fly into the rips, switched the rod to my left hand, and submerged my throbbing right elbow into the cool waters of the Kennebec. The current was a bit much, so I turned against it and waded shallower, bending lower so my ear almost touched the surface. Blissful, soothing relief. I zoned out for a moment, then looked up to see Sean's grin only a few feet away. He approached in his strong but measured Maine way.

"You do realize that you have a fish on?" he asked wryly.

"Well, sure," I lied, scrambling to play it to the net he was offering. "Hey, you know what? I think they're taking a caddis skittering on the surface!"

He released the brown, a pretty nice one at that, cataloging this incident with many others that day that might prove handy later on. A fish on, left-handed, behind my back, with the other elbow submerged so far I practically had my face in the water. It wasn't sunburn I was wearing.

"I won't mention this to anyone for the Chapter newsletter," he lied.

"You probably didn't realize I was a fish whisperer, did you?" I asked him.

We drifted on into the evening, Sean acquainting us with parts of our river that we'd never known. Just at dusk, I managed to coax a landlocked salmon over to my hand, admired it, and let it go.

Kathy Scott

By early July, we were immersed in life on the farm in Michigan, extended family, old friends, familiar haunts. In my case, and I know that I'm lucky, I can go home again. Granted, David and I own the house where I grew up, and my parents have gone different ways, Dad just around the corner on another part of the farm, Mom usually in Florida but home in the summer to visit, both happily married to stepparents I love. My siblings don't fill this house with teenage life now, but my sister is just a few miles away, my younger brother has driven up from North Carolina, and my older brother will always be here in spirit - we'll visit his grave before we leave. Out the window, the sweet sounds of Northern Michigan, of a family farm turned ranch, once crops and myriad pets and livestock now ranging beef cattle. Different, yet the same. Sometimes I have to pinch myself when I wake up.

Coyote songs lofted on the summer breezes floated through the open bedroom window this morning, but the pups were barely interested. We all drifted in and out of the music until the singers changed, the fluted wooden melody of the sand hill cranes, notes up and down the scales. Snuggled in a literal puppy nest, my eyes still closed, I pictured the cranes flying over the paddock and then over the hayfields, descending with great graceful wings, stalling, and stalking to find the insects, leopard frogs, and meadow mice amidst the stubble.

Other voices in the morning chorus cooed and chipped until the last moments of sleep ebbed away, mourning doves on a branch of the big maple tree I used to climb, chatty barn swallows executing precision dives then joining their cousins on the barnyard wire. Rock doves, pigeons, cooed at the top of the white silo and higher yet on the peak of the gambrel end of our classic red barn, centerpiece of the farm. Fledgling crows begged in the yard, distinguishable from their exploited parents by their red tongues and feigned helplessness.

The plan for the day was simple, tire out the pups, then go fishing. Early on, Effie and Midge learned the difference between "do you want to go for a ride?" and "do you want to go for a walk?" Their preference was clearly for the walk. By eight a.m., it was already eighty degrees, so a morning walk had to be the first order of business. The evening's ample dew still weighed heavy on the alfalfa. Spray followed the pups as they tore off through the fields.

Dad has been hauling big round bales from all of these field, seventeen at a time, so there were parallel trails from the tractor and wagon wheels packed by the weight of eight tons of hay. I followed one side of the pair that led down the big hill behind the barn directly toward the west while the pups played chase as satellites. The distinctions between these fields are subtle now, a matter of spotting clues in the types of grasses or contours, but these were once rotated through small crops of corn, oats, occasionally wheat, as well as hay and pastureland when I was growing up. Now that Dad ranches, the fences are down and the fields blur together, rolling green hills currently dotted with the remaining bales and surrounded by woods.

The forests, too, have subtle differences, easier to distinguish when aided by childhood memories. The maples along the line fence to the north shelter a wetland thick in winter with cottontails, raced after by the long line of beagles that accompanied my youth. A large swamp which herons frequent hid a fort for many years, a secret place sheltered in the embrace of maples and a few tall oaks, good trees for climbing. Those trees fade into an old hayfield that the neighbor, the boy next door, has revived. There's a large bale, his, near our fence.

Directly west, our back hayfield struggles to stay separate from encroaching brush dominated by volunteer apple trees that the deer have seeded. A shagbark hickory extends above the alders nearly hiding the old railroad grade. A winding path of woodland follows the intermittent creek, somewhat outlining the south side of the field, hiding banks covered in hand-picked stones, the unintentional riprap of farmers clearing fields. David and I loaded some of these rocks on the two-wheeled wagon while Dad drove the small tractor before he switched to a no-till process for seeding. On beyond this field to the west lies the lake, well hidden from view but sure to emit the sounds of summer play as the day progresses. As a teenager on horseback, I explored more than one friendship with kids vacationing from their city lives.

The pups' game of chase melted into a curious trot. They panted their way from sniff to sniff as I made my way across the back field. Effie followed the winding path of trees over each and every small stone pile until she emerged in the southern lobe of the field and a lone sand hill crane took flight. There were never sand hill cranes here when I was a child, what an exciting addition to the farm. We three paused to watch it fly, the long wing flaps, the incredible woody call, Effie, Midge and I. Then, as a test, I called the pups to my side, so amazed when they actually responded that as a reward I sent them off again.

Of course, that's exactly when I heard the tractor and turned to discover Dad driving down the big hill toward us. I needed to reassure myself that I could call Effie and Midge away from those wagon wheels and exert my power before he could arrive. Glancing around, I saw no pups. Of course not, I grinned to myself. I was just about to test my voice on the wind when I heard the crane. It was standing, squawking, on the big bale just over the fence, half a field away. As I strained to look, it seemed to shake its head at something, trying to see it better, maybe?

Effie. She was sitting about fifty feet from the bale, head and shoulders just showing above the alfalfa. She was cocking her head, too. The crane responded with that indescribable melodic sound and hopped off the bale, an easy jump for a five-foot bird but scaring Midge out of hiding and to my side. Effie stayed seated, and the crane explored the stubble. Two steps, three, four. That was enough, and I had Effie back, too.

Since David would be driving, which meant negotiating the infamous white tail deer gauntlet after dark, he'd foregone the walk. We found him appraising yesterday's flaming on the culms of cane he'd earmarked for three new rods. I recounted the odd behavior of the crane while we loaded our gear in the truck. We coaxed the pups into the basement where we hoped they'd appreciate the earth-bermed air conditioning as the day progressed. It was too hot for fishing, but we knew we could poke around the Au Sable area until evening without too much trouble.

The South Branch of the Au Sable has been our home river since our college days when we came to hike the sandy trail running all along its wooded shores the length of the Mason

Kathy Scott

Tract. That this section was and would remain protected from development seemed a promise we could count on. Many such promises, though, come with loopholes these days, and an attempt was being made to find one that would allow resource extraction within earshot of the river. Although we'd been aware of the existence of Rusty Gates and his Gates Au Sable Lodge, we'd never felt his presence quite so intimately as this year. His picture had been in the Detroit paper the day we crossed into the state. We made straight for his shop to catch up on the news.

"This isn't over until it's over, and we've a long way to go," Rusty told us, mischief behind those reassuring eyes. "We have court cases lined up and some very good arguments behind us. I was just in a conference call with all the partners."

Rusty is the president and foremost spokesperson for the Anglers of the Au Sable, a conservation group ready for a fight, a good fight. We first heard its voice as a loud objection when a major monetary gift was offered to the Michigan Council of Trout Unlimited by a huge international company (well known in Maine for pumping groundwater). There we no strings attached according to the water bottling company, and also according to the Michigan State Council of TU, long a champion of conservation. TU always has more worth while projects than money. It's the principle, the Anglers cautioned, follow the money and watch out for what happens next. The Anglers of The Ausable took the simple route by announcing the contribution and reaction was quick to come. Ultimately, the money was not accepted though not without hard feelings - change comes hard - and Rusty and his group regrouped.

The fight had turned to opposing both an exploratory well to be located within the Mason Tract and a remediation discharge to a headwaters stream, Kolke Creek. Rusty filled us in on all the details while we explored ways that we might help. He also offered enough hints about the evening's potential fishing that we finally pulled ourselves away and headed toward the stream, our home river and, thankfully, his.

We found our way through the sandy woods road to an uninhabited pull off beneath tall oaks. We stepped into our waders with the approval of nodding orange and yellow columbine. The path down to the stream was narrow and well-worn, our footfalls sending up diminutive clouds of dust to ankle height. Tiny blue and yellow forget-me-nots under a sweeping cedar reminded us how lucky we are as we stepped into a bend of the South Branch. Not likely we'd forget.

It was still pretty hot, but a peaceful walk in the cool waters helped, refreshing us and our casting arms before the evening hatch. We hadn't had our rods out in a few days, not since taking an informal census of the bluegills and largemouth bass in Dad and my stepmother Sue's new farm pond, now in its third year. At three acres, it's much smaller than the lake adjacent to the back field where they own nearly a half mile of frontage. It was easier, though, to make a pond nearer the house than to move the house, barns, stable, riding arena, and road access back there. The pond was a long time dream of Dad's coming true. Its bluegills were hand-sized already, and the bucket mouths, though more like thimble mouths, were a respectable seven inches long. Scrappy, too. We had released them all evening under rose and purple clouds, horses grazing in the paddock, deer grazing near the pines. This might be the only pond in Michigan that has only been fished with cane - Dad's old Montague and the rod David made for me.

No bluegills in the South Branch, though, no fish at all if our success for the first hour was any indication. We weren't fishing seriously yet, just wading upstream. If our timing was right, we'd be by the angler's chapel just about dark. I'd never fished that section of the river, but with the threat of drilling at that site, I needed to feel for myself what that might be like.

The last fly of a fishing trip must be chosen carefully. The memory of the evening floats on its shoulders, the last impression of the day. I chose something new, tiny, black for visibility to the little trout I hoped would find it, a bright white post so I'd know it if they did. The light had dimmed past my chance to try another when I cast to the side of some bright water beneath the chapel, the trees rising cathedral-high right above it, above me, above the water. I took it on faith that the tug on my line would be one of those Iron River strain brook trout, long ago grown wild, their sides so full of color it's as if the deepest, richest sunset has been embodied there. This one and three more were exactly that. There may be some trouble in paradise, but it is still paradise.

Our immersion in Michigan continued, but never long enough. The natural complement, we thought, would be to continue the trend by concluding the summer in Maine, getting to know our other back yard better. The question was only where to go? The coast is beautiful, but accessible in short weekend trips. The North Maine Woods could be explored for a lifetime. With an ample block of time at hand, we decided to head in, guided only by a whim. We've often heard on the evening news that Clayton Lake set the day's record as the coldest place in Maine. It was time to find Clayton Lake.

Sunday, August 22

There are basically three ways into the North Maine Woods, all of them through paper company checkpoints leading to their private and remarkably passable dirt roads. The tricks are two: don't get lost and listen for the overloaded log trucks. The tree length timber piled high, towering well above legal limits on public roads, gives the log trucks the undisputed right of way. If we entered the woods from the South, driving north past Mount Katahdin and Chesuncook Lake and on up to Caucomgomoc Lake, we could explore on through and come out to the East at Ashland or to the North in Allagash, near the border with Quebec.

Days later, we were walking Effie and Midge around the shore of Allagash Pond, making Clayton Lake an easy next day's ride. The pups had been infinitely patient, and we'd explored the North Woods with complete and satisfying freedom. Baker Lake had been on our list of places to see for ourselves since we'd first picked up canoe paddles; now the pups had finally splashed us with its waters. In fact, we made the decision not to drive on that extra day; why not save the mysterious Clayton Lake for another time and explore the pond at hand instead? There's something very liberating in just the freedom to change your mind, independent and unfettered. Something very North Woods. Fun.

Kathy Scott

Compared to Baker Lake, the headwaters of the St. John River and a fly-in starting point for many canoeists who choose not to explore the woods roads before their long and secluded river trip, Allagash Pond was a quarter the size. Both are small compared to their neighbors, lakes measured in miles, not acres. Baker Lake looks wild, shallow, and reminiscent of a northern pike lake in the great middle north of Canada. Allagash Pond is another kind of wild, Northern place, bouldered with granite, surrounded by mosses, stunted birches, and fir. Someone of whom we were immediately envious had a cabin, a camp to Mainers, on the north end. We'd decided to walk over.

The North Woods breeze had a nip to it already in August and sparkled the pond with enough waves to persuade us to leave the rods behind. If we had fished every pond that looked this promising, we'd have stretched our trip to months. Instead, we gave the day to Effie and Midge, and they explored every rock and fallen log. We kept them directed toward the old camp, making our way along an aging trail complete with a slippery boardwalk wherever there was water or fragile plant life but falling to neglect. Creeping snowberry and twinflower decorated the mosses; circular gray lichens adorned the rocks.

The camp appeared to be intact, although its roof wouldn't be for long. Probably a single room, maybe a partition for a bedroom, an outhouse but piping for water from a spring (pushed above ground from too many winters of frost and inattention), and, most important, a covered porch the width of the camp facing the pond. We might have lingered there ourselves, but the pups were suddenly on alert. Since we couldn't locate the object of their attention at first glance, we pulled out leashes, gathered and secured them before investigating. We suspected it was more than a squirrel by their posture and felt immediately guilty about snooping around the camp, although in these woods, that's usually welcomed as visiting rather than suspected as trespassing. Still.

Effie and Midge strained away from us as we tried to lead them back along the trails, hopping between rocks, negotiating the boarded sections. Underneath the boards, the signs of snowshoe hare were sprinkled on the moss. This wasn't far, as the adult lynx travels, from the study area covered by Mark McCollough, the endangered species biologist for U.S. Fish and Game. With so much prey in evidence in these northern forests, it's no surprise that he's found many lynx, their chief predator. Not far from here, too, one of the many "last wolf" sightings in Maine had occurred last year. We were as excited as the pups by the time the huge bull moose stepped out of the dense cover. It waded deep into Allagash Pond, submersing its great head to nuzzle for aquatic morsels. Probably the people on the porch of the camp had passed hours watching its ancestors.

Kathy Scott

Tuesday, September 13th

The pups followed me single file across the new meadow of pioneer plants which used to be the Big Pond. Tall grasses and plants I'll have to key out obscured our footfalls across the new, pathless territory, the sunken logs and remnant stumps which once scraped the bottom of our canoe now gray-white and threatening to trip us. Where the way was clearer, we walked on dried peat the color and texture of a paper wasp's nest although much more substantial. With the natural demise of all of the downstream dams, the character here is much changed.

Nearer the Hilton Brook, a small stream again after years as a fast current in the beaver pond, the peat grew dark and moist, but still cracked into deeply patterned splits, any exposure to air far drier than its submerged former life. We found a shallow pool in the stream, the footing there secure and boney enough to cross on the rocks. Along the west side, we followed what had been the shore of the pond, the easiest footing just at the newly exposed edgeland. The beaver lodge rose high above the grasses, access channels now dry and clearly pointing to the hidden doors. If I crawled inside, what would I find? Sleeping platform? Grooming station? I glanced at the pups. Mice, therefore snakes, black water snakes? Mink? The pups would probably follow, potential trouble, and I'd need a headlamp anyway. I might fit, though. It was worth considering.

Changing Planes

A blue heron flew up from the direction of the Hilton, hidden across the flat meadow. We three watched its silhouette against the dark pines, then we continued north, the pond oddly silent. Last year, its rippled waters were the stopping point for hundreds of geese and ducks. Now, instead, there were waves of grass over drying peat and the silent tracks of deer and moose.

We continued our great clockwise circle, moving closer to the jetties, the remnant arms of the Big Dam had breached two years before, the last dam below them finally conceding defeat last Spring. A loneliness settled over me at the sight of a small swamp maple beginning to redden, the first hint of Fall. It could be a very different autumn without these ponds.

It's hard sometimes, the coming of autumn, with aging parents and life moved on and the farm and family and friends and places West both missed and off limits until next summer a year away. Hard to see through the blur, a little hard to see ahead when things are changing, have changed. It makes little sense for us to own part of the family farm in Michigan, but I wouldn't have it any other way; there is something there worth preserving. We were going to spread Kodiak's ashes on the beaver house, but we've kept them instead in a Shaker basket rodmaker George Barnes made for us, to be mixed, maybe, with our own someday. Hard to let go.

The pups had stopped behind me, and, thinking of Kodiak, I felt their absence. I turned just as the objects of their attention flushed, a flock of wood ducks, two dozen or more, rising and crying to us from somewhere near the jetties.

Two dozen!

Kathy Scott

With no water near their boxes this season, what an amazing sight.

Then black ducks, four, followed. We three hurried toward the jetties. What water was there for so many ducks? Then literally dozens of mallards and some ring necks, an extended sound wave of ducks lifting off. How could they all have fit in the stream?

The answer was at the jetties. The pups led the way through the tall grass to the breach and stopped, I thought, to avoid walking in the trickle. No. No trickle there. Mud, sticks, a small new dam, maybe six inches high and stretching from jetty to jetty, mud packed by expert paws.

A new beaver dam? I had thought it might take, at best, five years for depleted food sources to grow, maybe longer to attract beavers back. It still might. But here it was, a tiny beginning, a rebirth.

I nearly cried, not sad, not really. I just didn't realize that I missed the ponds so much, the old beaver who lived right here but seemed so frail the last time I found him downstream, the hundreds of fall ducks, the evenings of moonlit geese. Not back, true, not the same, but something. Acceptance that the past is past, recognition of a certain promise. Funny how they conspire.

We crossed on the new sturdy pathway, a good solid foundation. A small start, but a substantial one. A single goose flew past - it had last night, too - the mate of one of the three lost last year? I fought back the sadness of that wounded goose calling all last November, alone each time a passing flock departed until the coyote came. Cycles. It's all about cycles. Life goes on, hope. New things, old things reborn.

"Don't worry," I whispered to the goose, "I think it'll be okay."

Kathy Scott

I have really come to believe each of these rods
not only carries the spirit of the builder,
but it goes deeper than that.

~ Glenn Brackett

Changing Planes

Saturday, October 16

Sitting, sorting, by the woodstove fire tonight, and sharing memories as I put things away. It has been a month or more since the rodmakers gathering in the Catskills, but those moments are as real as their paperwork and the dunnage I'm putting away.

Some day, we won't miss the feast on Friday night at the Roscoe Motel, Tom Smithwick's chili, George Barnes' homemade cheeses, the accompanying kick-off party. Until then, it's just nice that such a little motel in such a peaceful small town stays open until eleven when we finish the eight-hour drive, and that a hardy and hearty handful of rodmakers stay awake to wave us in. That first night is wonderful but a bit sleep-deprived.

The next morning on the shores of the Willowemoc is a different story. Always, I'm too excited to sleep in. We pause every year at the Esso Station across from the Roscoe Diner, where we used to find Poul Jorgenson each morning. With ice in the cooler, we follow the winding river to the narrow bridge, drive across to the museum, and join the growing crowd for breakfast. Willis Reid, Kim Mellana, and Ken Gaucher started this gathering; Chris Bogart and Jim Krul planned this year's, the tenth anniversary, with Jim Wilcox and Gordon Koppin.

I found a place in the cupboard for the gathering's coffee cup bearing Kim's commemorative art. She had decorated the pavilion with caricatures of rodmakers and scenes of that first gathering: John Zimny who advises us on thread, Al and Carole Medved and their bulldogs Bo and Osh, reelmaker Gary Dabrowski, and our cane importers, Eileen and Harold Demarest. Everyone pictured had touched me, touched my rod in some way. So good to see them all again. Dennis Higham, who had once advised me to savor these gatherings. As much as the classical rodmakers were often friends and collaborators in the past, he said, this next generation of rodmakers is making its own history. Bill Harms, half-smoked cigar in hand, is working on a book as a tribute to his mentor, Vince Marinaro - always say thank you.

This year, we'd met Catskill tyer Mary Dette Clark's grandson, Joe Fox, while standing under a likeness of Massachusetts rodmaker, now gone, Digger Degere. I'm just getting to know Mike Canazon, first house on the left from the museum. He looks like a surfer, acts like a Trout Bum, and has the heart of a rodmaker. The Canadians, those light-hearted makers of exquisite fly rods from the Canadian Cane gathering, all drove down. Near the likeness of Hoagy Carmichael had stood Hoagy himself. He had lunched next to David and me, and I had finally found a chance to say thank you for the Garrison book, thank you for the taper for my rod. He had been kind enough to ask to see it, and we had talked of Atlantic salmon in Newfoundland and Labrador while he looked it over. Before we left, I had thanked Al Medved, too. After all, it was a rod of his making that had inspired mine.

Changing Planes

Carl Cote had driven down, our Maine friend who'd taken the summer class, and compared progress with his cane classmates. Back in Maine by the fire, it's fun to know that we have a kindred cane spirit nearby. He'll be indispensable working with the Atlantic salmon babies, too. Carl knows Maine waters.

David, tonight, is mostly here with me, sorting things out, although I know that a little part of him is smiling more about this morning than the gathering last month. Today we bought a tractor with a 6-foot wide, rear-mounted snow blower and a front loader. Let it snow.

Thursday, March 2

Light snow just started, pretty, gentle. The pups have given in to the heat of the wood stove and are stretched out, Midge on the floor, Effie on her bed in front of the glass doors. David is wrapping the guides on the butts of Jeff and Steve's rods; he dipped their tips for the second time last night. I finished forty more leaders to take to Minnesota, so I should have some rod time soon. Since the March we lost Kodiak, the Great Waters Expo has captured my allegiance with its great heart and persuasive conservation message. Tom Helgeson has given a forum to a growing crowd dedicated to stewardship of the Driftless Area, a place glaciers never touched that I need to explore. Helping it, being a part there of things pretty much sight unseen, has become important to me. People there have become important, too: Jerry Kustich driving over from

Kathy Scott

Montana, but also tireless Duke Welter, poet Larry Gavin, and rodmaker Don Schroeder, whose cane I would only hear of in reverent conversations otherwise, and many more, rodmaker Dave Norling, Bob and Lisa White. Bob's rodmaking still life hangs near my rodmaking bench. My Midwest fly fishing community. Pick up a fly rod, my childhood schoolmate Kelly Galloup told me, and the world gets smaller. Amazing to find him again in Minnesota; he must be right. Still, I'd love to work on my own rod – it's like a constant ache.

Anyone making a split cane fly rod should be well aware that assorted constraints could get in the way, or they will weigh heavily. I was; I knew full well what I was facing, but I also realized that no one would be timing my progress. I certainly wasn't going to be.

In retrospect, though, it is easier to see what has happened. Setting aside the hours spent at work, the time required plus the extra time necessary to actually do things well, plus the hour commute as a price one pays for living at the edge of the North Woods, plus continuing the after school time with the fly fishing club (just when Alex Miller graduates, his brother Sam comes along; just as Chase Fabian is about to graduate, his brother Codey comes along), setting aside all those, say, twelve hours a day, leaves another twelve for sleeping and everything else. In reality, there might be four or five to play with. Dedicate at least two of those to the pups, as much a pleasure as a necessity if the sleeping hours are going to be effective, and that leaves two. Chip away at chores like the wood pile or snow clearing, allocate time to be the president of a Trout Unlimited chapter or a representative to the Atlantic Salmon Federation, visit or call parents. The list can and will always be long, especially for people who embrace their lives. Still, as I suspected from the start, I wouldn't change a thing.

Besides, there are plenty of those little steps to do that don't need much time.

A rod sack may be a little thing, but ordering mine from Classic Sporting Equipment in Vermont gave me a chance to include Bailey Woods in my rod. I'm beginning to think of my rod as a symbolic community; it takes a fishing village to make a split bamboo fly rod? We visited Bailey once to watch him work, years ago, his shop and methods as nice as his classic hardware.

My ferrules were made by Minnesotan Tony Larson, size 11, or eleven sixty-forths of an inch, the diameter of the blank where the ferrule is to be mounted. We had also visited Tony and Pumpkin, Darlene Urbanski, feasting on rodtalk as well as thick wedges of pie. Besides several ferrules, we picked up the planing form I used to make my tip. While we were there, Tony gave me a large spool of rich, thick, golden silk thread; I'll be furling a length of it into a lanyard for my ferrule plug later on.

In order to assure a smooth transition to the cane of the rod, I decided to feather and sculpt the tiny metal tabs on my ferrules, much as David does. He showed me how to use a jeweler's file to delicately round each little square tab, one after the other. I worked the file carefully into the dividing slot and tried to mimic his technique.

Mounting the male and female halves of the ferrule in turn on a small drill rod allowed me to carefully sand their tabs thinner. Although I'd pretty much decided not to wrap mine with a thread that would leave them visible, I had a different cosmetic in mind. The feathering would allow for a graceful climb of the thread from the cane up on to the metal of the ferrule. Once varnished, the wrap there often appears to crack, probably from the stresses of casting. Although I doubt this affects the performance of the ferrule or of the rod, I hoped to avoid the cracking just in case. It looks nicer.

When the ferrules were ready, David brought out epoxy for me to measure and mix. He found a wooden block while I retrieved the dental floss. I scratched the inside of the male and female halves of the ferrule where they would contact the cane, scoring them for better bonding with the glue. We'd played these roles with every rod he had ever made, so this was familiar ground even if this rod was mine. He dabbed glue into the end of one of the ferrule halves, pushed it onto the cane until the air bubbles popped out, then I held it firmly against the little block to keep it seated while he secured it with floss. With the second half of the ferrule, I dabbed the glue, popped out the air, and wrapped the floss, just to make it more mine.

Another small step, I dug through the bag of cork rings spilled over my workbench near the woodstove, sorting out the 1/4" thick disks I'd want for my grip. I had measured my hand against the grips on the various rods in the house, settled on a length, and tried to find enough relatively pit-free rings to build it. Using wood glue, I smeared the facing sides of three and secured them between large washers on a threaded bolt, stacking trios to grip length. When the glue dried, I tested the trios in their order along the blank, then drilled the interior diameter to match that point on the taper of the rod, more or less. It's easier to drill three at a time than a whole grip.

I need to wrap the ferrules and finish gluing the grip next. When I can. A certain peace comes from realizing that there is no reason to rush, that good craftsmanship, like a good, well-lived life, takes time. For now, I wiped another coat of Tru-oil on the blank.

One of the puppies is snoring, Effie. Midge is lying with her head across her sister's shoulders, cute. I can hear the gentle revolutions of the overhead fan. The woodstove is cooling just a little, clicking randomly as the cast iron adapts, small sweet noises only a little louder than the soft crackle of the slowly burning logs.

Saturday, March 11

The pups' spring fever was contagious today, so we were all out exploring the Hilton in the fresh, warm morning sun. David and I found caddis in wooden homes, one with stripes and especially interesting, while the pups sought moles and over-wintered bones now liberated from what little snow we had had this winter. Buy a tractor, we joked, and that's it for snowfall.

Effie and Midge retired afterward while we drove up to check on the salmon incubators. They were still heaped with the snow the Atlantic Salmon Commission guys had hauled in and piled up to insulate them, another irony after all the work we all put in last year, digging down through deep snow to find the incubators and change the filters. Some of the snow had melted to reveal the piping, but water still ran freely out the exit, so we were satisfied that all was well and left them alone. We lashed a treat and note in a waterproof bag to the waiting shovel.

After traveling on to Rangeley, we drove on to the Oquossoc store for pizza. Oquossoc, Abenaki for Arctic char, blueback trout, now lingering in only a handful of Maine lakes we discussed over lunch. Then we circled south around Rangeley Lake to check out South Bog Stream, where State Biologist Forrest Bonney had worked with a Trout Unlimited Embrace-a-Stream grant. We wanted to see the restoration work, but we also wanted to decide if the informational kiosk there was simple enough to copy for our ASF grant for signage on the Sandy, an Atlantic Salmon Federation - Trout Unlimited partnership. Without signs, we reasoned, unwitting anglers might think that the brown trout parr were especially numerous while actually catching little Atlantic salmon from the incubator project. With any luck, they might also catch what would appear to be a monster brown, really an Atlantic trucked up from the new Lockwood Dam lift, a channel-fed, 1,800-gallon hopper and 2,500-gallon holding tank system with a guaranteed ride from our on-call ASC friends Paul and Dan. If any Atlantic salmon came to the Lift, if any salmon came up the Kennebec – we'd soon see. A few signs here and there could be very helpful.

Changing Planes

While walking the pups again in the afternoon, we marveled at the changes since morning. A day pushing fifty degrees speeds spring closer. The stream ran higher, more difficult to cross, and the marshlands were considerably wetter with the redistributed melt water.

Toward evening, David showed me how to wrap my dark green YLI size OO silk on the feathered and scalloped tabs of the ferrules and then coat it with rodmaking alchemist Mike Brooks' walnut oil concoction so that the threads wouldn't capture air bubbles when varnished. I hoped to avoid a white sheen.

I actually hoped to avoid wrapping the rod.

Maybe it was the trauma of those early rodmaking days when my patient and understated rodmaker-in-residence could be heard cursing under his breathe, or those explosive moments when he'd jump up and walk away for a while that did it, but I was more than worried about the next step. It didn't matter that David had mastered wrapping thread since then or that all of his rods were expertly adorned. This would be my first time laying thread on cane and I could find no miracle to save me from the torture of just going ahead and getting it done. I can re-wrap until the dawn of the next millennium, I told myself, if that's what it takes to get these right, but it wasn't an encouraging thought.

Of course, wrapping wasn't nearly that bad.

With the rod secured into place on my bench and the silk secured in the tough little bronze tensioning tool, I angled the thread across a flat, then rotated the blank while guiding the wrap around the cane and up the ferrule. Just a few revolutions before the end, I inserted a loop of a coarser thread. As I finished wrapping, I slipped the end of my silk through the loop, pulled the loop back out, and trimmed off the excess.

To smooth out the wraps, I burnished them, rubbing them flat with a white plastic tool David provided. That's when he showed me the overlapping threads about midway down the wrap, and I decided to pull the whole thing off. The next time, the adjacent threads weren't as tight together as I wanted, probably because I was intent on avoiding over-wrapping them. By off-setting the device so that the thread approached the blank at an angle, I reached the compromise David had assured me would happen.

Choosing the wood for the reel seat insert was made easier by our Upper Peninsula friend Jim Bureau. All of his inserts are so beautiful, it would be hard to go wrong. David pulled out everything from our cabinet, and I lined up my blank with the trios of my cork grip. We scrutinized each one for color and design, curly maple, striped maple, even alder, all from Michigan, all from home. Then we measured and cut the exquisitely figured black ash burl which would be mine.

The only other component which ornaments a cane rod as much as the wood of the reel seat is the stripping guide, traditionally lined with a red agate. I had other thoughts. Why not incorporate a bit of Maine? The rock bound coast and the mountaintops celebrate the gamut of colors of granite, one possibility; I'd have to ask about using granite.

Changing Planes

Tourmaline varies in transparent to translucent hues from pink to green to black. As Maine's semiprecious state gem, it was an interesting second possibility. David dropped by a backstreet rock shop which seemed our most likely source, bringing home a shaving of tourmaline we decided was too cracked to be useful. The shopkeeper also suggested Maine jasper, a blood red, but it appeared too grainy to cut to size. Finally, right across the street from Charles Wheeler's former cane rod shop, a Farmington jeweler cautioned us that good tourmaline, worthy of a stripping guide on a split bamboo fly rod, would cost half or more of the price of the rod. My practical side kicked in; that was the end of that.

Our alternative was to call guide maker Mike McCoy in Oregon. I'd be using his wire guides the length of my rod, deftly crafted and strong with guide feet so tapered that they accepted wrapping smoothly, no doctoring required. I looked at my rod with a different eye. What color agate would match the stunning dark mottle of the cane, the rich, deep browns of the reel seat insert? Black, maybe. Maybe a dark green like the thread I'd wrapped on the ferrules.

I'd never met Mike McCoy, but he had earned such respect through his work that I suddenly felt too embarrassed to call and inquire about colors. I accepted their importance, but I didn't want Mike thinking I was being stereotypically female, like caring more for about the color of a car than what's under the hood. David knew better, but I couldn't shake the thought so I did something even worse. I asked David to call. Fortunately for me and my somewhat irrational pride, he loves calling Mike.

Kathy Scott

Mike didn't have anything cut in green or in black, but he had a black banded green agate stone that was crafted and in our hands in under a week. It was perfect.

David went back to drilling the centers of his glued cork trios to better fit the taper of the butts for Jeff and Steve's rods while I worked on furled leaders for Minnesota. I'm anxious to hear about the collaborative work to protect and restore the Driftless streams in the adjacent areas of Minnesota, Iowa, Wisconsin, and Illinois; I wonder what I can do to help. I wonder, too, what my Midwesterners have been doing, how they are. I want to talk with Dr. Thomas Waters, a stream champion and former Michigander, like me. He's become another respected friend I almost never see. Since we last met, he has a new Brittany pup, Sara. Jerry Kustich will be sharing some space with me at the Expo, big changes in his life, Winston to Sweetgrass. Change for Ron Barch, too, a grandbaby due, and Tom Helgeson will be celebrating the engagement of his son. A few leaders an evening, my elbow just might make it this time.

Sunday, March 12

This morning's seamless sky has morphed into overcast so even at these, the warmest temperatures of the season, we're chilled enough for David to build fires in both wood stoves. The two pups are investing their spring-fueled energy in lying watch at the glass doors near the wrapping bench, apparently on guard for trespassing red squirrels also fueled by spring fever. When we were ready to open the front door after breakfast, Effie and Midge sat, stayed, shook hands, and then shot out on "okay" to scatter squirrels near a cone cache in the woods, but within sight. They seem to be mindful of their last scolding; we've had to step up the training a bit.

About a month earlier, we had finally timed it right to catch them red-handed and hot-footed, chasing a squirrel right out of the woods and into the path of an oncoming pickup. The pups never paused. With spring thaw in full swing, Mud Season, the road had fortunately become a barely passable mud and pothole obstacle course, so the truck was barely crawling and easily stopped. The pups ran on after the long-departed squirrel despite anything I could say or yell. Wild goose chases have nothing over tracking spring-insane pups. Once David and I finally gathered them up, I called L.L. Bean and ordered a training system, a micro, waterproof, two-dog 300-yard multichannel, single control for two collars system meant to save their lives.

I was a little worked up.

When it arrived two days later, we both were so worried it would break the pups' spirits, or hearts, or just scare them to death, that we put it aside. For now, the love and tasty treats method, along with some focusing rituals (sit, stay, shake, okay) before they rocket off, all seem to be working. Even on our walk today through heavy squirrel territory, they seemed to come back when we called. Mostly. Joie de vie, joy of life. Joie de squirrel? We'll keep at it.

Kathy Scott

Around lunchtime, David showed me how to clean my hardware with a silicone-free rubbing compound, then bathe it in acetone. Rodmakers tend to avoid silicone, any silicone encounter however remote and logically disconnected, lest the blank becomes contaminated and the finish won't adhere. I really like the look of a blued reel seat, so I finally decided to experiment. Better, in theory, to have decided before mounting the ferrules, but not too late.

The bottle from our bluing supplier Jeff Fultz said to clean the components with lacquer thinner, so we did that, too. I made myself a sweet potato, and David made a peanut butter sandwich while things dried, and we talked it through. Then it was time for me to go ahead. I picked up the bottle and tried to twist the lid off. Tried harder. Okay, false start; David twisted the lid off and handed it back, grinning. I'm starting to suspect that he does this on purpose to sabotage my intensity.

With the jar open, I looped string through each of the circular pieces, slide band, cork check, and stripping guide, and dunked them in turns in the solution. After timing each part for sixty seconds, I handed them to David to rinse in cold running water. I followed with the end cap, dropping it in the jar and fishing it out after sixty seconds with a lifter made from two coffee stirring sticks. I can always blue them longer if I don't like this look. The little knurls on the end cap didn't take evenly, so

I'll probably need to clean the rubbing compound residue out of each tiny space and then try again. The solder joints on the stripping guide Mike McCoy made me didn't take the bluing at all, but the look is really nice anyway. A good experiment, and well worth finding a way later to blue the ferrules already mounted on the rod.

David glued up a grip while I made more leaders. To rest my elbow, I'm sticking to five or less each time, but making them more frequently. While we worked, we talked about the details of the salmon signage grant, due Wednesday, and the upcoming cane class in June. I thought sanding blanks was next on David's agenda, but he dug out a Hardy reel, claiming that he hadn't cast the newest rod yet and at 51 degrees it was plenty warm outside, he'd better do it before it rains. I guess I'll have to help him.

Saturday, April 8

To better counteract any chance of impatience, I decided to make a list of the remaining steps before I can introduce my rod to water. April 1st may be the season opener, but my favorite stream won't fish until well into May. At this late stage, there's also no room for avoidable problems, the offspring of hurrying.

The cork trios need to be glued together and shaped into a grip, and I need to reshape a circular winding check into a hexagon so that it will slide nicely on to my blank. Before I progress to any more wrapping, I should double check the taper of the feet of all the guides to see if any feathering is necessary. To complete the butt, I'll sand the blank, varnish it, and repeat the process, probably twice, maybe three times. Then I'll write on the rod before varnishing, sanding, and repeating, until I apply the last coat. To fit the grip, I'll remove the reel seat, wrap the cork wrap, and glue the winding check in place. Then, there's the wrapping, signature wrap and stripping guide, followed by coating the threads, deglossing them carefully, and repeating that step. After the last varnish is dry, it'll be time to affix the reel seat and butt cap.

The tip will need similar sanding and varnishing, and then repeating those. Once the guides are wrapped, I'll need to coat those wraps, degloss them, and repeat the coating at least twice. At the same time, I can glue on the tip top, wrap the interface between it and the cane, and coat that, then add more coats. Then, barring any ladybugs crawling up the wet rod or a pup sending it flying with a wagging tail, there will only be the final varnish to go.

Seems like a plan.

Changing Planes

Monday, April 24

The 1/4-inch cork rings that I had selected and glued into pairs or trios, then pre-drilled so the center holes would match the diameter of my rod, I mounted tonight on one of David's mandrils, a long screw. He'd left it covered in adjacent bands of masking tape, wound in the decreasing diameters that would simulate the taper of his last rod. I peeled each one of them back to approximate the taper of my rod, testing it with the cork. Then we coated the tape with pump-spray oil. I threaded a spacer on the mandrill, then I smeared the inside flat of my most pit-free cork with glue, Titebond II, and strung it on the mandrill next. I coated one flat of a cork trio and rotated it snugly into place against the first cork. The rest followed.

While I retrieved paper towels and cleaned my hands, David slipped on the washers, which would act as protective spacers, and a long nut. After he tightened it a bit with a box end wrench, just a bit of glue squeezed out at each joint. I wet a paper towel to wipe it off, then another, and a final towel, until the grip was ready to set for a few hours. The exteriors of the corks are a bit mismatched under pressure, but the lathe will take care of that. Some rodmakers sand the grip to shape right on the rod; I thought it best to minimize any risk of damage to the blank. Working just with the cork would be awkward enough.

The wings of woodcock are singing this evening as they spiral up into the night.

Kathy Scott

Saturday, May 6th

The "raw" grip looks pretty ragtag. I had pulled it off the mandrill, borrowing time from rod work for a few days, then reinserted the mandrill so I could chuck up the grip in the lathe. Using Al Medved's rod as a model, I shaped it slowly with sanding screen and sandpaper. When the belly reached my target diameter, I worked the front of the grip smaller but gauged the back bigger, sanding it less. The final sanding completed the progression from screen to 220 grit paper, then 400. Satisfying to watch the steps go by, almost ready to hold the blank, almost a fly rod, time to see how the grip and reel seat would look on the blank. Exciting.

A tease, of course. The grip wouldn't slide onto the blank. A look inside revealed the problem, though, so I wrapped sandpaper on a dowel, inserted it in the grip, and twisted it until the interior space was free of wayward glue.

Then I slid it into place.

Committed again to patience, I slipped on the reel seat (it did look beautiful, a nice match), then measured the blank just in front of the grip to determine the winding check size. Measured in 64ths, like the ferrules, my little rod probably needed an eighteen. I'd helped David shape round checks into hexes, so I felt justified digging through the stash first to see if there was one already formed that would fit. One of them slid on just loose enough to allow for the threads of the eventual wrap under the check, but I decided to wait to blue it until the wrap was done and I could be sure.

With the reel seat, grip, and a winding check temporarily in place, I rotated the blank slowly. The flaming was mottled, a look I like but certainly not how Everett Garrison would have done it, maybe classic Michigan maker Paul Young. I picked out the most blond facets, two, side-by-side. They were just light enough to write on. With a fine-tipped archival pen, I practiced on a pencil, experimenting with lettering, with style, with the amount of information I thought I might want. Then I lightly sanded the entire blank to a dull finish. On the lower of the two facets I'd chosen, I carefully penned 6'9" 3 wt G193. Just above that, on the other facet, I wrote my name and then added maker.

Sunday, May 7th

During the night, we closed the bedroom window against the wind driven through by the high pressure cold front. At 45 degrees, this morning sparkled; so did my rod blank when examined in the morning light. Yesterday, with the pups sleeping, we had lowered the butt of the blank into the tube of finish, extracted it slowly, then followed with the tip, a relatively quick experiment to see how the spar urethane would take after so many coats of Tru-oil.

Kathy Scott

I thought that I would like the ease of applying the Tru-oil compared to the difficulty of a perfecting a traditional finish, but after three coats, I could see little wipe marks on my rod. Apparently, perfection isn't easy with the short-cut method, either. David, on the other hand, maintains that the incredible mirror-finish he keeps getting is very easy to do. Although I know it is for him, having helped for years, I was not so sure it would be for me, just like I pretty much dread wrapping my tiny tip guides. Still, why not try it and see? Thus the experiment to see if I could switch after three coats; would the spar urethane cover Tru-oil?

Apparently, it works well.

We discussed the various options for the next dip after rousting the pups for a walk along the trail to the south. The former Grass Dam was now the biggest in the system, extending one hundred-feet long and rising six-feet high. The South Pond has risen behind it, a small lake by many standards, reminiscent of the Big Pond of years past.

The first wild oats decorated the pathway, the fresh greens of spring suddenly noticeable. The winds must have blown the pollen away to tolerable levels, and the slight chill had grounded the blackflies. Both added to my enjoyment of the morning, I'm sure, but I suspect that the success of the dip contributed as much.

I crossed the dam to the far side without falling in, Midge following; Effie shadowed David across the series of smaller downstream dams just north. On the west side, the beaver had counter-moved where I had excavated by filling my channel with dried sticks piled high to slow the flow. Each piece it used had over-wintered and was as dry as kindling, cut with a scalloped point at each end. They played a woody melody as I tossed them aside into the growing pile.

The water rushed through again, down to the small dam David was dismantling. I scraped the bottom of the pond leading into the channel with a handy stick turned tool until the fines washed down and more ends were free, pulled out those sticks, and scraped again. We deepened more channels until it seemed likely to keep the beaver well-occupied with repair and, with any luck, allow the neighbor's lawn hidden across the ponds behind the alders a chance to dry out. No sense in escalating a situation with the neighbors.

The pups passed out after a great game of chase. We decided to take advantage of their nap: tire out the pups, then continue the rod work pup-free. I dulled the finish on my blank, just barely, and dulled the finish on the ferrule by using a thin strip of sandpaper around the round part and a sanding stick on the flat. Fifteen hours had passed since the first dip, plenty of drying time at this stage.

David placed the clear tube of spar urethane in the warming sun of the sliding door, tucking it behind the bamboo shade so the pups couldn't knock it over should they revive too soon. When the sections of the blank were ready, we secured the dip tube into place on the side of the bench. Using the hook on the pulley-supported cord, we caught the loop I had taped on the very end of the ferrule of the butt and manually lowered that section until the surface layer of the thick liquid was just even with the top of the ferrule wrap.

I switched the little clock motor on, then watched the butt slowly rise to the hum of the motor and the gentle clicks it makes, a reminder of both its origin in a clock and of the amazing passing of time. It's just over two years since I started this rod.

After we inserted the tip section, David blotted a bulge of urethane from the end of the hanging butt. When the tip was hanging beside it, two beautiful rod sections shining in the morning light, we decided to leave them to dry in peace. We packed up the pups and loaded up the fishing gear to push the season a bit.

Wednesday, May 17

Each evening inches the rod forward at a pace that would probably have given me the heebie-jeebies if I hadn't know it would be this way. Admittedly, I could cut some corners now, but I want this rod to be as good as I can possibly make it, something that doesn't diminish David as my mentor in the eyes of anyone examining it. Besides, I want to fish it for the first time at the right time, when the fishing is at its best, say, mid June. Easily a month away.

Last night, the walnut oil treatment, Mike Brook's Stuff, was dry to the touch on the cork wrap. I tried the size 18 winding check. Too small to fit over the wrap, glad I hadn't blued it. We couldn't find a 19 that was a hexagon, so we pulled out the long tapered hexagonal tool and a rubber mallet. I slid a circular check up until it was a bit snug, and David showed me, once again, how to carefully tap one side and then the opposite side. Lying on a cedar shingle, the tool became the shaper of the little flat sides, rotated painstakingly until the ring became a hexagon. To smooth the sharp edges, we sanded and filed them down and then filed the interior edges. We finished the check by rubbing it on sandpaper to make it flat.

Then I slid it down the blank. It fit.

We cleaned the new check in acetone and dried it. Then I suspended it on a string and dunked it in bluing until we both liked the color. I rinsed it in a glass of cold water and blotted it on a paper towel. When it was dry again, I moved it to a piece of cardboard and sprayed it with clear lacquer. By then, it was nine o'clock, the chorus of spring peepers and the clucks of wood frogs filling the night.

Friday, May 19

The toads are trilling now, their mating call and a serenade to the pups on their walk before bedtime. We timed our afternoon walk between showers and were treated to a rare clap of thunder just before a suppertime torrent. Only a month or so before we'll be on the road to Michigan, where thunderstorms are fantastic. We didn't see the young moose again today, the why-doesn't-my-mama-still-love-me gangly adolescent that has been hanging out in the road near the house. Poor thing, twice unlucky, driven to the road for a breeze to escape the black flies and displaced by this year's calf.

We juggled the numbers in Frank Stetzer's on-line Hexrod, software developed by Wayne Cattanach based on math by Everett Garrison, a Wisconsin - Michigan - New York collaboration across time as well as space. With Hexrod's help, we compared the guide placement designed by Garrison for this taper rod with the guide placing Al Medved used on the rod we own and love. Garrison put three guides on the butt; Medved put two. I liked the thought of two, but noticed that the stripping guide on Al's was beyond my reach. I needed my rod to fit me if I'm holding the grip with one hand, touching the guide with the other. David helped me with the pros and cons of changing the guide spacing increment with the stripper as the index, virtually moving the other guides closer to the ferrule and the tip, until we settled on the best choice for me.

Saturday, May 27

It rained lightly, drippy, in the night, and the air is thick and too warm already today. Mosquitoes were active when I walked the pups at five this morning; Midge was so occupied with their electric bites that she forgot to do her business. The pollen isn't much friendlier. Effie and Midge and I have retreated indoors, where the nuisances of the season still seek me out at the most inopportune times.

Changing Planes

When I decided to wrap my guides in silk, I tried to pick the color YLI thread I liked the most. Since, I reasoned, all of the colors of the same thread would perform the same way, color was a cosmetic choice. I've never been handy with cosmetics or fashion of any kind, but I thought that wrapping a variety of colors of thread on a sample section of bamboo would give me an idea or two. Unfortunately, they all looked good. The dark flaming of the bamboo tied in nicely with the black ash burl of the reel seat insert, and a dark brown, dark burgundy, dark green, or black matched well. So did medium shades of earth tones. Red looked better on rods that weren't flamed, I thought. So did lighter green.

David suggested a color that would appear clear, or a lighter brown, but both reminded me of his rods. While the greatest compliment I could imagine would be to have my rod mistaken for one of his, I thought that so unlikely that I wanted to be distinct enough to avoid any chance of confusion. My rod, my mistakes. But, partly as a thank you to him and partly because I liked the look, I decided to go with a dark green thread. It would tie in the green agate in the reel David gave me for my birthday.

When I mentioned to George Barnes that I was finally wrapping my guides, he said, "I hope you're using a light color."

"David suggested that, too," I confessed, "but I liked the dark green."

David just smiled.

"You know your rod will show up more between those dark wraps if you don't get them close," George said.

Oh.

Newly enlightened but still committed, it wasn't until nine last night that I wrapped my second guide, the last one on the butt. The first took a while. It would have gone better if I hadn't tried to secure the end of the thread by pulling it back through wraps so close to the guide that it came unraveled. I rewrapped it, but I may have crossed one thread. I tried it again; the close work is hard to see anytime, worse with pollen everywhere. I finally wrapped the other foot on the stripping guide and called that one good. David and the pups shouldn't have to be subjected to a longer bout of my intense mood and concentration.

To see if it might help, we switched the rod end-to-end on the wrapping stand so I could work directly under my light, David's idea. If I leaned in close, I could see fairly well. He also tried to show me just how easy it is to start a wrap, again, but it just wasn't easy for me, period. One of those things, I told him, that I know I'll look back on one day and wonder what was so hard about it, but until then, irritating. Still, after immersing myself in it for an hour, I had the next guide wrapped on, a #2 at that. By then, my eyes were nearly swollen closed with allergies. I coated the wraps on the feet of the first guide with a dab of varnish on the end of a small knitting needle, and David saved me the frustration of trying to see the wraps on the second.

Tuesday, May 30

The rainless days of spring extended the snow free days of winter into a long dry season, perfect for varnishing rods, not so perfect for our watershed. The brook retreated into its deepest channel, in places so narrow the pups and I could jump across. The level of the South Pond lowered despite the beavers' efforts to raise it and with no sympathy for ours to lower it, the dam providing a high and dry route across to the western shore. Frogs, tadpoles, and turtles shared extremely close quarters; minnows were constantly stranded as side channels diminished to isolated pools, then vanished. Only the straw colored marsh grasses rivaled the acres and acres of exposed peat for its tinder-like flammable condition.

Still, I didn't expect a fire.

Last evening, I drove up the hill, a gentle curve, and pulled even with the first driveway at the north house before I saw the crowded fire trucks, pickup trucks, ATVs, sooty firemen and hustling volunteers, all shrouded in smoke. With every bit of the clearing filled with trucks and activity, I squeezed into the fray, firefighters focused and in motion. I climbed out and into their midst, forcing a quick visual survey.

What was burning?

No flames from the house. Effie and Midge were in their usual window, not barking, just watching the show. The house must be safe. Sheds? No one over there. David, where was he? I approached the nearest firefighter, outfitted for combat and intent on retrieving something from the truck. His face was serious.

"Excuse me," I managed, "This is my house. What's up?"

I thought I composed myself rather well.

"Oh, man," he said, apologetically, "No one told you? We should have a sign or something."

Maybe I was a little shaken, maybe not, but I had no idea what that meant. Before I could think of what to respond, David came around the house. He seemed a bit wide-eyed.

"The pond's on fire," he said, half shaking his head. "Or, what was the pond. I noticed fog down the hill when I walked the pups over here so I could finish some planing. I thought it was odd, so I stashed them inside and came back out to look just as the flames took off. So I called the Sheriff."

He paused to share a smile, inside joke. We're the very last community in Maine without 911.

"These guys came fast," he continued, "and just in time. The first truck pulled in right when the fire hit the trees below the house. If they hadn't been here, it would have raced up the slope. Feel that breeze behind it?"

I did. I could also feel reality turning my knees to rubber: if David hadn't been here, the pups and the house would be gone.

We watched from the top of our hill as men, smoke, and flames materialized here and there.

"I told them it was okay to drive the ATVs right to the stream and pump water directly from it. It's a lot easier than trying to get a truck down there."

The fire warden arrived during the cleanup, stepping with us over charred logs and acres of scorched peat, some hot spots still flaring. We three walked the perimeter of the fire with her GPS mapping its area, all of us speculating about the potential cause. Causes. Who knew? She'd arrived late from a fire scene in town, a case of spontaneous combustion in a fast food restaurant's flower bed. Certainly there were combustible materials here, too, or a piece of errant glass exposed from its discard and long years resting on the pond floor. No one had been present, at least not to our knowledge, no shell casings, no cigarette butts, no clues. We looked at the adjacent dried peat lands over the jetties, the long brittle marsh grasses, the acres and acres so similar and as yet unburned. We both forced back that feeling of vulnerability, but our situation was obvious.

Some of the firefighters, neighbors we didn't even know, lingered over hot spots until nearly dark, then left us portable water canisters and a caution to keep close watch on the deepest peat for a month or so. Smoldering coals could flare up in a breeze anytime. Then we were alone, dousing three more hot spots with our giant department-issued squirt guns. It was oddly beautiful, black as coal as far out as the stream, dotted now and then with glowing orange smudges or sudden fingers.

Alone but not alone. There's nothing like volunteer firefighters for rekindling a sense of community. Although we chose to live in a relatively secluded place because we embrace the outdoors, we counted again the fortune of many cooperating hands. The cane community, the conservation community, those who rescue and care for foundling dogs, those who rescued us.

"I wish it would rain," I told David.

"I thought you were going to say that after all that work you were glad your rod was safe," he teased me.

"Well," I grinned. "that, too."

Friday, June 16

Just east of the beaver lodge, the Big Pond had swollen from nearly a straight month of rain to a vague resemblance of its former glory. Instead of acres of lily pads, there were bright green grasses, more of a rice paddy look, replacing the dry peat bog look before the fire. The rain began that night and had barely paused since then. Watch what you wish for, we'd laughed, soggy. It seemed more of a rebirth than the usual spring, more than just water stretching beyond the bed of the brook.

On this morning's romp with the pups, the first day of my summer vacation and the last day of scheduled work for David for two months, I heard mink frogs. Hut-hut-hut, unmistakable. Deep water frogs, usually, not marsh frogs. They were between me and the lodge, on the east side. There is an impending sense of loss when a detail that has become so important is threatened, as the mink frogs were when we discovered the more aggressive green frogs on the west side. We accepted that; the green frog's twang was a natural part of the chorus. Then, the chinook, the breaching of the dams, and the long agonizing draining of the ponds gave us an extended meadow along a brook. We thought the mink frogs were gone. In time, we not only discovered an interest in meadow life, highlighted by the unexpected arrival of sand hill cranes, but we found remnant beaver lodges, evidence of past repetitions of this cycle. Then there was the fire, and a sense of wonder set in; how will this all play out? Then the rains. Then a moose, a displaced adolescent driven into the breezes of the meadow by mosquitoes, standing right in the place where we once watched its predecessors so often we called the water Bull Moose Cove. And today, cooler, sunny, and a small but persistent chorus of mink frogs.

And my rod is done.

Needless to say, wrapping my tip went better. With each guide, practice upon practice, the initial anchoring of the thread became easier. I measured the length of the wrap on one foot of each guide, then matched it on the opposite foot, practicing winding down one foot then up the other foot since the feet require mirrored attention.

Looking at the cane, I wish I'd been more aggressive in sanding the tiny flats of the tip between coats of varnish, but I opted for the security of good coverage over the cosmetics of sharp corners. The flats were still quite obvious for affixing the very tiny tip guides. I lined them up with the other guides, so the resulting rod is fine, but next time...

Using the small pink knitting needle, I coated each wrap on each foot, bracing my hand and taking pains to go slowly for thorough coverage but not overcoat or overflow on to the cane. After the third coat, David made me a sanding stick, a thin wooden coffee-stirring, mini-tongue-depressor, dressed in double stick tape and 600 grit sandpaper sliced to fit. Without touching the blank, I carefully dulled each wrap before coating it again. The winding check wrap was too fine for my still suffering eyes, I decided, so David coated it for me.

While the wraps dried, we prepared the butt to accept the reel seat by wrapping it with masking tape in two places to build a tight fit with the black ash burl and still allow an in-between space for the excess glue. At the last moment, I slipped a hair each from Effie and Midge into the center hole of the wood insert; it somehow seemed right.

I used a bamboo shish kabob skewer dabbed in epoxy to coat the ring, the cork check which fits against the cork at the heel of the grip, then coat the butt of the blank to accept the wooden reel seat insert. David looked on, busy scoring the inside of the metal cap. I had cringed while scoring the beautiful wood to accept it, even though I knew it would be covered by the cap. I'm starting to feel a bit protective of the rod, I'm afraid, ill-founded or not. We've been together a long time. When he finished preparing the cap, I slid the metal slide band we had blued onto the wooden insert, then glued on the end cap. Grip, cork check, insert with band, end cap. Almost done.

With the wraps completely dry, I carefully and in turn submerged the butt and then the tip in the long tube of clear amber, switching on the clock motor to raise each one slowly and in turn toward the vaulted ceiling. Tick, tick, first the butt, finally clear of the tube and then drying from the door frame, then tick, tick, the tip following in kind. My first complete split cane fly rod, hanging to dry, finished, now, except for a last detail.

Since it was late in the process when I had decided to blue the hardware, the ferrules were still waiting, a final touch. When we could, David showed me how to clean off any varnish with a strip of sandpaper, and he opened the jar of bluing again. We were both curious how this would work since he'd only blued ferrules before mounting them. The trick would be to dip them evenly with a section of rod attached.

We each decided to try one so that we'd both know how.

I braced my elbows and lowered the butt of the rod until the ferrule and meniscus agreed and held it there until the color seemed right, then he did the tip, the male ferrule taped off to the length of its fit.

Kathy Scott

When we had rinsed the ferrules and they had dried, I carefully applied a spray coating of spar urethane to match the rod. Next time, I'll blue them first. For now, of all my long list, I needed only to lap them. I waited until the next night to be sure I was ready, that I wouldn't make a mistake and overdo it, but they required only minimal work with a strip of sandpaper. The rod was ready for lawn casting. I went first, then David. It cast well.

The next morning, we took my rod to school and cast it again with Hutch in the high school gym, our usual tradition with a new rod. It still cast well. It took a bit to sink in. We were casting the rod I'd made, and it still cast well; I posted my relief on the rodmakers' list serv and then took my rod to meet Mike and Linda at the fly shop.

Today, David is making me a statistics sheet of all my rod's details.

Young beaked hazelnuts are loaded on the bushes along our paths; the last moccasin flowers, pink lady's slippers, are going to seed. The phoebe has started a second brood in the nest recently vacated by the fledglings, a new clutch just over our front door. The pups are watching their world awaken from their round denim bed, the tag chewed off. Well below their perch on the deck, a pair of geese. The lone goose has found a mate; they're nibbling the fresh shoots of green transforming the charred area by the stream. The sky is dawning an endless blue. There are no mosquitoes, no black flies, here on the deck, just a gentle breeze and memories of whippoorwills calling back and forth last night when the clearing was flashing with fireflies. Summer.

Changing Planes

Monday, June 19th

Three days, and I still hadn't fished my new rod. My own rod, the Hardy reel birthday present from David, a silk line from Olaf Borge who'd passed many an hour sitting on the tailgate of our truck, and my own furled leader. I was waiting for a perfect time, a perfect setting, a storied place and experience. The water was still high everywhere; we speculated that it would be so high in the Kennebec that the Lockwood lift would fail to attract Atlantic salmon, if there were any salmon swimming upstream. At least high water meant a chance for safe passage for the salmon smolt traveling downstream through the gauntlet of dams. Too much water for me to chance fishing my little rod, at any rate. We drove over to the conclave of the Flyfishinginmaine.com crowd with Hutch and Carl, and I shared the casting of it all around, finally on water but still without a fly. The people were special, but the first fish needed to be special, too, and I had a place in mind.

With a forecast of severe thunderstorms with damaging hail, you'd think we might have passed on the evening drive to Little Labrador, our code name for our favorite mountain stream. But our only concession, after persuading ourselves to go, was to linger in Rangeley long enough for some assurance that those severe winds probably wouldn't strand us with blow downs across a tote road. Then we headed in.

Kathy Scott

The thunderstorms in the back country had morphed into a steady rain, which should have kept any normal black fly down, but, true to its nickname, Little Labrador had plenty. We'd seen this many in the real Labrador, but they had been gracious enough to retreat in rain. Not these. We sat, waiting, at the ideal place for an hour. After I directed him in turning the car around on the tight two-track, David went out to check whether the hordes which had followed me right back to my seat had been replaced. Their cousins drove him back. The rod was directing our thoughts, obviously, because our solution was just to try a different perfect spot on the same stream.

At a wide bend between waterfalls that we call Jeff's Pool, the first place fished of another rod David made, both the rain and the black fly clouds did seem lighter. I geared up. Clever bugs; they were just waiting at the water. Black flies immediately started gnawing under my bug repellent shirt, with their midge reinforcements burning my forehead just below the brim of my bug repellent hat. Both attacked my casting hand. I should have tried DEET, but there was no way I was going to risk damaging the finish on my rod. I should have retreated, but I'd waited long enough.

One cast. The second the caddis touched the water, a bright wild brook trout grabbed it and ran hard into the quick water. I lost it. I lost two others, too, before switching to a fly I could actually see in the twilight. An even larger trout grabbed it and flew broadside out of the water and back in again and gone with me high-sticking in frustration before I realized that something was wrong. I examined the end of the rod. The line was knotted securely around the tip top. I noticed blood on my hands as I untied it, took a breath, and cast once more. There it was.

David and I took turns using the rod, catching and releasing beautiful little brook trout until we had to scramble back up the mountainside to the car in the dark. I was nearly frenzied with pain, popping a Benadryl with a Diet Coke chaser. David lifted a Sam Adams, a Sam-D.C. toast. We clinked and headed out.

The first moose, we easily missed. The second, a big, frantic adolescent, leaped out of the bug-filled brush to the relief of the more open road and what we assumed was a sure collision with our car, but David and the moose braked hard, and it was a standoff instead. The moose seemed mesmerized by our headlights and wouldn't move until it finally decided to run down the narrow road in front of us. We followed slowly until we could aim our headlights into an opening, a gravel pit, and the moose ran in. We turned off our lights, waited, and it was gone when we turned them back on. The rest of the road out was a gauntlet through red-eyed snowshoe hares, then the highway was shrouded in fog. Still, we were home by midnight, when the antihistamines knocked me out.

Not the outing I'd planned, but fun. And the rod worked.

Kathy Scott

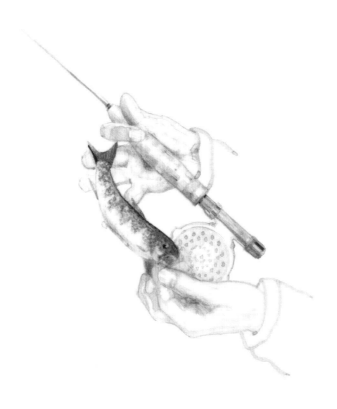

A fly rod extends a fly fisher's being
as surely as do imagination,
empathy, or prayer.

~ David James Duncan

Changing Planes

Sunday, October 1

My new little cane rod danced through a gentle cascade of fishing, family, and friends all throughout the summer and into the fall. Not the last trip of the season, though. I retired it as a new friend and invited along instead the cane rod I had always fished, at least since that day David pronounced it finished, his first rod, my old friend. The familiar nostalgia of fall stirred wistful feelings once again. How hard some changes can be but how inevitable. Whether the passing of an aging companion followed by the total occupation of foundling puppies, the realization of a missing part of a riverine ecosystem and the personal investment to restore it, or simply the change from rodmaker's assistant to maker of a split cane fly rod, a safe and comfortable plane may well give way to a different plane, equally comfortable and as infinitely interesting, if only approached with an open mind and heart. Sometimes, not always, it's possible to have both. What is the old rhyme? Make new friends, but keep the old?

We found our way north though the logging road maze to a secret place, one of those places guides share only with the promise that you'll check with them before potentially intruding there and that you won't mention to a soul. No lip service to this promise. I swear. We had checked in advance to see if our friends would be there on the last day of season. One had taken us with him two years earlier, and we hadn't ventured near the place again. But he was guiding elsewhere this year, and the other was out of the state, so the place was ours. We resolved to turn around if anyone at all was at the parking place before the long walk in. We looked over our shoulders as we drove deeper into the North Woods.

The last trip of the season with my new rod was special, although this wasn't that trip. Our friend Bob Dionne had invited us to fish two weeks earlier, a trip to a tiny and as yet elusive headwaters lake that fed Little Labrador. He didn't have to ask twice. We'd been defeated in the search for that lake a few times already by a combination of unmapped trails and a greater motivation to explore other waters. We'd meant to go back all summer, but a change of planes had continued as a theme; we both tried some new things.

We had traveled to Michigan, as usual, to spend time with the family. After testing my rod at the South Branch of the Au Sable, our usual haunt, we invited Ron Barch to join us for a day at my father and stepmother's new farm pond. The bass they had planted were three years old. Dad drove his ATV across the rolling hills while the rest of us walked. The low evening sun danced on the waters, on the grasses, on the purple blossoms of alfalfa, through the flowing manes and tails of the horses grazing nearby. David and Ron had released several fish before I had even lured one to my fly. Dad and Sue and their dogs stood on the arching bridge over the narrows of the hourglass pond, watching, giving advice.

"You cast like you're fishing for trout," Dad told me. "Tie on something noisy and splash it down."

Changing Planes

Changing planes, I dug out the biggest Chernobyl ant my little rod could maybe handle. I'd fished for bluegills and smallmouth in ponds, but I'd never tried largemouth bass and I'd never been so skunked. I pulled out some line and slapped the fly down. In that one spot, my little rod found twenty-nine fish on twenty-nine casts, the last with only one leg of the ant still tied on the hook.

Then we packed up the pups and tried Colorado.

The rodmakers' gathering out at Spruce Tree Ranch was new for us. Each gathering has its own character and characters, and we found these rodmakers as wonderful as those at the Canadian Cane, Catskill, Penobscot, and Greyrock gatherings. Some were old friends met elsewhere over various years, like Ralph and Pat Moon, and others who were virtual friends, like Jeff "The Gnome" Hatton. Darrol Groth and Dave Collyer demonstrated cholla cactus grips, not something we'd see in Maine. I studied Alan Kube's rod wrapping demonstration. Doug Borer offered me a tiny black nymph to try with my rod, which worked very well. I thought one of Lee Koch's bamboo nets would be nice too, maybe some day. We met too many rodmakers to remember all their names. Afterwards, we visited with veteran rodmaker Mike Clark and his cane wrapping counterpart Kathy Jensen in Lyons, where Mike showed us Kathy's first rod handmade from the culm, and they both offered excellent fishing advice. My little rod found greenback cutthroats, browns, even a brook trout. A new state, new people, new fishing. About then, we started missing those things familiar, and drove for hours just to fish our favorite Wyoming stream for a joyous day.

Kathy Scott

On the actual way home, we stopped to explore new water, the Driftless Area of Minnesota, and to lunch with Tom Helgeson. We were getting the hang of it. Changing planes was good, but it didn't mean that the old planes were lost or even set aside. Sometimes, you can have it all. We lingered in Michigan as long as we dared and then returned to Maine. We just missed the official ceremony and the breeching of the Sandy River Dam in Mercer, but we drove over to listen to the music of the rapids at the dam site, singing again after too many years. Then we accepted the invitation from Bob to find the headwaters of our Little Labrador.

Bob drove. A light-hearted spirit, guide, and outfitter who always finds time for the good parts of life, who else in the North Woods of Maine would name his shop after an aardvark? My new cane rod and David's, the first he's ever kept for himself, were in the back seat with the other gear and David. I rode up front, not really the navigator. It was to be a group effort, but Bob had come close earlier and could almost smell success. I smelled something else, but not until we'd ridden a long walk from anywhere.

"Are we on fire?" I asked. "Just curious."

David smelled it, too.

Bob was jovial, enjoying the adventure of it all.

"Oh, that's nothing. There's a hole in the floorboard under my floor mat. The muffler's probably getting hot and melting the rubber. Look, I think we go this way!"

It wasn't that easy, but we did finally find the pond, a shallow reflecting pool ringed in black spruce and apparently lifeless. We launched the canoes unperturbed. If willing brook trout into these waters could make it so, they'd be there. We paddled in tandem then veered apart to cast our cane. One. Two. Three. Brook trout as colorful as those from storied waters, just like that. They were everywhere, just invisible against the trout colors of the shallow bottom. We could do no wrong. Bob tossed his fly back over his head to let it rest while he solo paddled to a different spot and had one on. Time ran out before the fishing died down. We switched rods right at the end so Bob could try mine. It worked for him, too.

And then it was September 30th. We'd considered Little Labrador, an old friend. We'd considered its headwaters pond. But in the end we retired the new rods and turned down a different path, a little farther to drive, a little less certain, but we were excited. A change.

Why no one was parked at the gate across the logging road, I don't know. Luck. How we found the landmark to cut off into the endless spruce, I don't know either, and I imagine it was only the down slope and not our keen memories after two years that led us right to the river and to the place we called September 30th Pool. The meander was as moody as the weather, the water cold, grey clouds promising flurries before long.

"I feel like an Atlantic salmon," I joked, "returning finally to a place that I barely remember."

"Fifteen caught in the Lockwood lift and transported to the upper Sandy," David reminded me. "Did you hear that the DNA results are in? One was our baby."

I stopped midcast. "For sure?"

There was no doubt. One had beaten the incredible odds. There was no need to think beyond that; one was enough for the moment. Just four years since the project began, an adult salmon had actually come back.

I fished the rod David had made for me, its familiar grace satisfying in this wild, remote pool, a setting so mossy and moosey that it was an honor just to be there, a deep joy that such a place could still exist. I didn't anticipate much luck beyond the tiny eager brook trout at my feet, nothing like the trophy our guide friend had caught and released here two years before. I had never fished to big fish and didn't really know what to do. At the moment, I didn't really care, either. The nip of winter was in the air and this special pool was reward enough.

I flicked my little streamer, a Woods Special, to the opposing bank. A lively little trout nailed it and attempted an exciting run. I nearly had it to my feet when it made a unique twisting escape. I managed to play it near again, taking care not to horse it in. I didn't want to hurt the last trout of the season.

Then it went rushing past my feet sideways. My eyes registered the sight, but my mind couldn't wrap around what was happening. My line did start to wrap around the little brookie, my little trout and a relative giant that had clenched it in fierce kyped jaws.

Changing Planes

Oh, man!

David not only had time to wade over, but to stand and consider with me while the battle continued. We couldn't think of a thing to do. No camera, of course, the biggest brook trout of my life not hooked and certainly not likely to twist up in the line enough to stay caught if it decided to let go. My net was on my back, but what would we do with it? It was a brook trout net, to be sure, but meant for my usual small stream variety fish. Not a chance it could help.

I decided that the best I could do would be to save the life of the little brook trout. I waved my hand close to the battle, and the impressive specter disappeared.

"You have no idea how lucky you are," I told the little one as I let it swim from my hand.

We were both quiet on the journey home. We didn't get lost, we were just thinking. Changing Planes. Would I be crossing over, measuring my brook trout in pounds not inches? Hard to believe, I love small streams, but maybe both. If a fly rod is a window to another world, a look at trout like this could be interesting. David appeared to be concentrating on the road. Really, he was reading my mind, smiling. Big trout, someday, maybe Atlantic salmon. There was no need for either of us to say it; we'd shared the joke so many times.

How many cane rods do you need?

One more.

Kathy Scott

Acknowledgements

*C*ane rodmakers and conservation advocates. I hope that these pages read, in part, as a tribute to them, as well as to all the other caring individuals whose paths have crossed with ours. Some names could have slipped by; that doesn't mean that the appreciation is any less, just that time and space have conspired a bit.

A few people for special mention and thanks:

As always, David Van Burgel, but also Ron Barch and Kim Mellema. Without them, this book couldn't have happened.

For his sage advice and unflagging support, Tom Helgeson. Jerry Kustich always finds time to lend a hand despite the miles between us. For their kind words, too, Mary Dette Clark and Bill Townsend. Beyond the context of this book, all four of them have earned my greatest admiration for their continued good works.

Thanks to Susan Morris, Norma Stankevitz, Dean Baker, and the rest of Lawrence Junior High; to our friends and our familes; to Carole Barch and Willis Reid; to Jeff Wagner, Dave Patterson, and Mike Holt for early thoughts and forgotten details; to Dan Marra (the next chapter president); to biologists Paul Christman, Dan McCaw, and Jason Overlock, for their inspirational work.

Anyone who has shared a good life with canine companions will understand the great debt I owe to Kodiak, and to Effie and Midge.

- Kathy Scott